INTERNATIONAL THEOLOG UMMISSION

THE RECIPROCITY BETWEEN FAITH AND SACRAMENTS IN THE SACRAMENTAL ECONOMY

*All documents are published
thanks to the generosity of the supporters
of the Catholic Truth Society*

Cover image: Disputation of the Holy Sacrament *c.1509-10 (fresco) by Raphael,* Apostolic Palace, Vatican City. Wikimedia Commons.

This edition first published 2020 by The Incorporated Catholic Truth Society 42-46 Harleyford Road London SE11 5AY.

Libreria Editrice Vaticana omnia sibi vindicat iura. Sine eiusdem licentia scripto data nemini liceat hunc The Reciprocity between Faith and Sacraments in the Sacramental Economy denuo imprimere aut in aliam linguam vertere. Copyright © 2020 Libreria Editrice Vaticana 00120 Città del Vaticano. Tel. 06.698.45780 – Fax 06.698.84716 Email: commerciale.lev@spc.va

ISBN 978 1 78469 649 8

CONTENTS

4

4. THE RECIPROCITY BETWEEN FAITH AND MARRIAGE. 93

PRELIMINARY NOTE

In the course of its ninth quinquennial, which has been extended exceptionally by one year due to the celebration of the fiftieth anniversary of its foundation, the International Theological Commission has been able to deepen its study of the relationship between the Catholic faith and the sacraments. This study was directed by a specific sub-commission, chaired by the Rev. Fr. Gabino Uríbarri Bilbao, S.J., and composed of the following members: Msgr. Lajos Dolhai, Fr. Peter Dubovský, S.J., Msgr. Krzysztof Góźdź, Fr. Thomas Kollamparampil, C.M.I., Professor Marianne Schlosser, Rev. Oswaldo Martínez Mendoza, Rev. Karl-Heinz Menke, Rev. Terwase Henry Akaabiam, and Fr. Thomas G. Weinandy, O.F.M. Cap. The discussions on the subject in question, on the basis of which the present document has been drafted, have taken place both during the various meetings of the Sub-Commission and in the Plenary Sessions of the same Commission, between the years 2014-2019. This document, entitled Reciprocity between Faith and Sacraments in the Sacramental Economy, was specifically approved by the majority of the members of the International Theological Commission during the Plenary Session of 2019 through a written vote. The document was then submitted for approval to its President, His Eminence Cardinal Luis F. Ladaria Ferrer, S.J., Prefect of the Congregation for the Doctrine of the Faith, who, after having received the favourable opinion of the Holy Father Pope Francis on 19th December 2019, has authorised its publication.

1. FAITH AND SACRAMENTS: RELEVANCE AND ACTUALITY

1.1. THE DIVINE SALVIFIC OFFER IS BASED ON THE INTERRELATIONSHIP BETWEEN FAITH AND SACRAMENTS

1. [*Starting from Scripture*]. "Daughter, your faith has saved you. Go in peace and be cured of the disease" (*Mk* 5:34). In the midst of the crowd that pressed in on him (*Mk* 5:24; 31), the haemorrhaging woman touches Jesus with faith and receives a healing, as a symbol of the salvation that Jesus brings to humanity.[1] The case of the haemorrhaging woman shows how faith springs from "the encounter with an event, a Person, which gives life a new horizon and a decisive direction."[2] Faith is located in the sphere of interpersonal relationships. Many sick people tried to touch Jesus (cf. *Mk* 3:10; 6:56), "for out of him came a power that healed them all" (*Lk* 6:19). However, in Nazareth he did not perform many miracles "because of their lack of faith" (*Mt* 13:58), nor did he satisfy Herod's curiosity (*Lk* 23:8). The humanity of Jesus Christ is the effective channel of God's salvation. However, this efficacy does not have an automatic character; it requires an adequate contact with it: humble, imploring, open to the gift.[3] All these attitudes lead to faith, as the most apt means to receive the offer of salvation. "Faith is first of all a *personal adherence* of man to God"[4] revealed in Jesus Christ. The sacraments of the Church prolong in time the works of Christ during his earthly life. In them is actualised the

---

[1] Cf. *Catechism of the Catholic Church*, 1116.

[2] Pope Benedict XVI, Encyclical Letter *Deus caritas est* (25th December 2005), 1: AAS 98 (2006), 217. Quoted again by Pope Francis, Apostolic Exhortation *Evangelii gaudium* (24th November 2013), 7: AAS 105 (2013), 1022.

[3] Cf. Origen, *In Leviticum hom*. IV, 8 (PG 12, 442-443).

[4] *Catechism of the Catholic Church*, 150. Underlined in the original.

healing power that emanates from the body of Christ, which is the Church, to heal from the wound of sin and to give new life in Christ.

2. [*And from Tradition*]. In the Trinitarian economy of salvation there is a rich intertwining of faith and sacraments:

Faith and baptism are, however, two mutually inherent and inseparable modes of salvation, for faith is in fact perfected through baptism, and baptism, for its part, is founded through faith, and both attain their fulness through the same names. For as we believe in the Father, in the Son and in the Holy Spirit, so we are baptised in the name of the Father, the Son and the Holy Spirit. And certainly the confession of faith goes forward, which introduces us into salvation, but baptism follows, which seals our assent.[5]

The personal relationship with the Triune God is realised through faith and the sacraments. Between faith and the sacraments there is a mutual ordination and a circularity, in a word: an essential reciprocity. However, as Basil testifies in the above text, confession of faith precedes sacramental celebration, while sacramental celebration secures, seals, strengthens and enriches faith. Yet today, in pastoral practise, this interaction is often blurred or even ignored.

1.2. CURRENT CRISIS OF RECIPROCITY BETWEEN FAITH AND SACRAMENTS

a) Faith and Sacraments: A Reciprocity in Crisis

3. [*Finding*]. Already in 1977 the International Theological Commission, referring to the sacrament of marriage, warned of the existence of "baptised non-believers" who demand the sacrament of marriage. This fact, they said, raises profound

---

[5] Basil the Great, *De Spiritu Sancto*, XII, 28 (SCh 17bis, 346).

"new questions."[6] Since then, this reality has not ceased to grow and to generate discomfort in the celebration of the sacraments. Moreover, problem is not limited exclusively to the sacrament of marriage, but embraces the entire sacramental economy. In particular, in Christian initiation, where by its very nature the reciprocity between faith and sacraments should be sealed, concern and uneasiness are often detected.

4. [*Theological-philosophical roots*]. Although the disassociation between faith and sacraments is due to different factors, according to social and cultural contexts, a look that does not want to remain on a superficial level must ask itself about the ultimate roots of this fracture. First of all, beyond possible shortcomings in catechesis and certain cultural unilateralism against sacramental thinking, there is a deep-rooted philosophical factor that destroys sacramental logic. An extended line of thought, starting from the Middle Ages (nominalism) and reaching Modernity, is characterised by an anti-metaphysical dualism that dissociates thinking from being and categorically rejects all kinds of representative thought, as is the case today in post-modernity. This perspective rejects the Creator's imprint in creation, that is, that creation be a mirror (sacramental image) of the Creator's own thought. In this way, the world no longer appears as a reality expressly ordered by God, but as a mere chaos of facts, which man with his concepts has to order. Now, if human concepts are no longer something like "sacraments" of the divine Logos, but mere human constructions, then there is a further dissociation between the personal act of faith (*fides qua*), and any shared conceptual representation of its content (*fides quae*). In short, and as a decisive aspect, when the capacity of reason to know the truth of being (metaphysics) is denied, the inability to gain access to know God's truth is being implied.[7]

---

[6] International Theological Commission, *Catholic Doctrine on Marriage* [1977], § 2.3.

[7] Cf. St John Paul II, Encyclical Letter *Fides et ratio* (14th September 1998) 84-85: AAS 91 (1999), 71-73.

11

5. Secondly, scientific and technological knowledge, which is so prestigious today, tends to impose itself as a single model in all fields of knowledge and for all kinds of objects. Its radical orientation towards certainty of an empirical and naturalistic type is opposed not only to metaphysical knowledge, but also to knowledge of a symbolic nature. While scientific knowledge emphasises the capacity of human reason, it does not exhaust all dimensions of reason or knowledge, nor does it cover all cognitive needs for a full human life. Symbolic thinking, with its richness and plasticity, on the one hand, collects and elaborates reflectively the ethical and affective dimensions of experience; and, on the other, touches and transforms the spiritual and cognitive structure of the subject. For this reason, together with all the religious traditions of humanity, the transmission of revelation, with its concomitant cognitive content, is situated in the symbolic sphere, not in the empirical and naturalistic sphere. The sacramental reality of participation in the mystery of grace can only be understood in the unity of this double dimension of the symbolic experience: cognitive and performative. Where the scientistic paradigm reigns, which is blind to symbolic thought, sacramental thought is obstructed.[8]

6. Thirdly, we must still point to a significant cultural change, proper to the new civilisation of the image, which poses a new problem to the theological clarification of sacramental faith. While it is true that rationalist modernity minimised the cognitive value of the symbol, contemporary postmodernity nevertheless exalts with great intensity the performative power of images. Thus, it is necessary to overcome the rationalist (modern) prejudice against the cognitive value of the symbolic, without falling into the opposite (postmodern) excess, which reduces the effectiveness of the symbol towards the emotional power of representation, empty of reference. In other words, Christian intelligence must preserve the originality of the Christian sacrament from the risk of

---

[8] Joseph Ratzinger. "Die sakramentale Begründung christicher Existenz," [1965], en *Gesammelte Schriften* 11. *Theologie der Liturgie*, Freiburg –Basel – Wien 2008, 197-198.

double emptying. On the one hand, there is a danger of reducing the symbol-sacrament to the status of a mere cognitive sign that just easily gathers the doctrinal meanings of the faith, without operating any transformation (elimination of the performative dimension of the symbol-sacrament). On the other hand, there is a danger of reducing the symbol-sacrament to the pure aesthetic suggestion carried out by means of its ritual staging, according to the logic of a mere representation that replaces the interior adherence to the symbolised reality of the mystery (suppression of the cognitive dimension).

7. [*Distortions of Faith*]. In today's societies there are other phenomena that make it difficult to believe, as proposed by the Catholic faith. Atheism and the relativisation of the value of all religions are advancing in many parts of the planet. Secularism erodes faith, and sows doubt, instead of fertilising the joy of believing. The rise of the technocratic paradigm[9] inserts a logic contrary to faith, which is a personal relationship. The emotional reduction of faith produces a subjective belief, regulated by the subject himself, which moves away from the objective logic marked by the contents of the Christian faith. This culture of scientism, already mentioned, tends to deny the possibility of a personal relationship with God and his capacity to intervene in one's personal life and history. The objectivity of the Creed and the stipulation of conditions for the celebration of the sacraments are understood, according to an increasing cultural sensitivity, as a coercion of the freedom to believe according to one's own conscience, managing an insufficient conception of the freedom one intends to defend. From this type of premise, there is a kind of belief or way of believing that does not fit into the Christian conception or correlate with the sacramental practise that the Church proposes.

---

[9] Cf. Pope Francis, Encyclical Letter *Laudato si* (24th May 2015) esp. 106-114: AAS 107 (2015), 889-893.

13

8. [*Pastoral Failures*]. In the post-Vatican II period, there have also been some widespread attitudes among the faithful and pastors that have actually weakened the healthy reciprocation between faith and sacraments. Thus, the pastoral approach of evangelisation has sometimes been understood as if it did not include sacramental pastoral care, thus losing the balance between the Word of God, evangelisation and the sacraments. Others have not grasped that the primacy of charity in the Christian life does not imply contempt for the sacraments. Some pastors have focused their ministry on community building, neglecting the decisive place of the sacraments for that purpose in this endeavour. In some places, there has been a lack of theological evaluation and pastoral accompaniment of popular Catholic piety in order to help it to grow in faith and thus achieve full Christian initiation and frequent sacramental participation. Finally, many Catholics have come to the idea that the substance of faith lies in living the Gospel, despising the ritual as alien to the heart of the Gospel and, consequently, ignoring that the sacraments impel and strengthen the intense living of the Gospel itself. The need for an adequate articulation of *martyria*, *leitourgia*, *diakonia* and *koinonia* is therefore pointed out.

9. [*Consequence*]. Not infrequently, pastoral agents receive the request for the reception of the sacraments with great doubts about the faith intention of those who demand them. Many others believe that they can live their faith fully without sacramental practise, which they consider optional and freely available. With different but widespread accents, there is a certain danger: either ritualism devoid of faith for lack of interiority or by social custom and tradition; or danger of a privatisation of the faith, reduced to the inner space of one's own conscience and feelings. In both cases the reciprocity between faith and sacraments is harmed.

b) Purpose of the Document

10. [*Purpose of the Document*]. *We intend to highlight the essential reciprocity between faith and sacraments, showing the mutual implication between faith and sacraments in the divine economy.* In this way we hope to contribute to overcoming the fracture between faith and sacraments wherever it occurs, in its double aspect: whether it is a faith that is not aware of its essential sacramentality; or whether it is a sacramental praxis carried out without faith or whose vigour raises serious questions regarding the faith and the intention according to faith that the practise of the sacraments requires. In both cases, sacramental practise and logic, situated at the heart of the Church, suffer a serious and troubling injury.

11. [*Structure*]. We take as our starting point the sacramental nature of the divine economy[10] in which both faith and the sacraments are inserted (chapter 2). We elaborate an intellection of the economy that includes simultaneously: the divine economy as such in its Trinitarian, Christological, Pneumatological, ecclesial and dialogical (faith) unfolding; the place in it, thus understood, of faith and of the sacraments; and the reigning reciprocity between faith and the sacraments that derives from it. This understanding constitutes the theological background from which the specific problem of the interrelationship between faith and sacraments will be approached in each of the sacraments that will be dealt with later. This chapter illustrates that a celebration of a sacrament without faith is meaningless, because it contradicts the sacramental logic that underpins the divine economy, which is constitutively dialogical.

---

[10] St John Paul II, Encyclical Letter *Fides et ratio* (14th September 1998) 13: AAS 91 (1999), 16, has spoken of "the *sacramental* horizon of Revelation" (underlined in the original). Benedict XVI, Apostolic Exhortation *Sacramentum caritatis* (22nd February 2007) 45: AAS 99 (2007), 140, takes up the central idea and refers to the "sacramental perspective of Christian revelation."

15

12. This will be followed by the incidence of reciprocity between faith and sacraments on some of the sacraments most pastorally affected by the crisis of this reciprocity, either in their understanding or in practise, as are the sacraments of Christian initiation (chapter 3). In light of the doctrinal elucidation of the specific role of faith for the validity and fruitfulness of each sacrament, we offer criteria for elucidating what faith is needed for the celebration of each of the sacraments of initiation. In a further step (chapter 4), we address the interrelationship between faith and sacraments in the case of marriage. By its very nature, we dwell on a question that the reciprocity between faith and sacraments could not ignore: the elucidation of whether the marriage union between "baptised non-believers" is to be considered a sacrament. This is a particular case, in which the articulation of the reciprocity between faith and sacraments in the economy is truly put to the test, as the second chapter maintains. It ends with a brief conclusion (chapter 5), in which, on a more general level, the reciprocity between faith and sacraments in the sacramental economy is taken up again.

13. [*Doctrinal Character*]. The intent of the document is clearly doctrinal. It is certainly based on a pastoral problem, differentiated for each of the sacraments dealt with. However, it is not intended to offer specific or grounded pastoral tracks for each of them. We wish to insist on the fundamental place of faith in the celebration of each sacrament, without leaving out the doctrinal precision on the case of the faith necessary for validity. From this, some general criteria for pastoral action can be extracted, as we do at the end of the treatment of each one of the sacraments considered, but without going into details, much less entering into casuistry or making up for the necessary discernment of each particular case.

14. [*Choosing*]. We are aware that the pastoral situation around other sacraments, such as penance and the anointing of the sick, also suffer from serious deficiencies. Not infrequently, full

participation in the Eucharist is sought without any awareness of the need for prior reconciliation with God and the ecclesial community, from which we have been separated by our sin and which we have damaged in its reality as the visible Body of Christ. There is dissociation between the Eucharistic life and the practise of reconciliation on the part of many faithful and even of some ordained ministers, ignoring in the practise of their Christian faith the harmonious unity of the whole sacramental organism of the Church, where it is not possible to *choose subjectively* which sacraments to "consume" and which to forego. The anointing of the sick is also often experienced surrounded by magical elements, as if it were a kind of spell invoking a miraculous intervention of God or of the divine Spirit, without a personal relationship with Christ, Saviour of the person, both of his body and of his soul. The limits of space force us to concentrate on those sacraments that make up Christian initiation and marriage, all of exceptional importance in building and strengthening the Body of Christ. The way in which these sacraments are approached, as well as the isolated allusions to the rest and the general theological framework that is offered will allow us to draw consequences for those sacraments that we cannot consider monographically.

2. DIALOGICAL NATURE
OF THE SACRAMENTAL ECONOMY
OF SALVATION

15. [*Introduction: plan and objective*]. In this chapter we make a double general incursion in order to discern the existing reciprocity between faith and sacraments. In the first section, we consider the divine economy, discovering in it a sacramental nature.[11] This allows us to deepen our understanding of sacramentality as a constitutive dimension of it. The treatment of sacramentality as such requires, by itself, a deepening of faith, thus highlighting the interconnectedness between faith and sacramentality and also, and more concretely, between faith and sacraments. We conclude this section with a recapitulation of the constitutive axes of the sacramental economy most featured in our exposition. This illuminates, in a first step, the reciprocity between faith and sacraments. In the second section, we pause to consider faith, on the one hand, and the sacraments of faith as such, on the other hand, showing, however, in both cases the intimate reigning connection between faith and sacraments. Faith is constitutively predisposed towards the sacramental celebration. The dialogical nature of the sacraments calls for an adequate faith in their celebration. Both sections of this chapter have a complementary tenor, which allows us to show both the breadth and depth of the reciprocity between faith and sacraments, with their various ramifications. The chapter closes with a brief conclusion.

---

[11] Cf. *Catechism of the Catholic Church*, 1076: "The Sacramental Economy." See note 54.

2.1. THE TRINITARIAN GOD:
SOURCE AND END OF THE SACRAMENTAL ECONOMY

a) Trinitarian Foundation of Sacramentality

16. [*Sacramentality: concept*]. To sacramental logic belongs the inseparable correlation between a significant reality, with a visible external dimension, e.g. Christ's whole humanity, and another meaning of a supernatural, invisible, sanctifying character, e.g. Christ's divinity.[12] When we speak of sacramentality we refer to this inseparable relationship, in such a way that the sacramental symbol contains and communicates the symbolised reality. This presupposes that every sacramental reality includes in itself an inseparable relationship with Christ, the source of salvation, and with the Church, the depository and dispenser of Christ's salvation.

17. [*Triune God: root*]. The understanding of sacramental logic presupposes an understanding of how the divine economy of salvation operates, which springs from the Trinitarian God, the communion of distinct persons in the unity of a single divine substance, and from the redemptive incarnation, in which the eternal Word, without detriment to his unrestricted divinity, assumes our humanity with all its consequences. This framework clearly affirms the presence of God himself in the humanity of Jesus Christ, the Word sent by the Father, who became incarnate of the Virgin Mary by the work of the Holy Spirit. The encounter with the humanity of Jesus Christ, anointed by the Holy Spirit for his public mission, is, through faith, an encounter with the Incarnate Word. It is with these keys that we understand how it is possible for a sensible, sacramental *word*, perceptible by us humans, to be simultaneously the true word *of God*. Human persons are only capable of perceiving, experiencing and

---

[12] "If we must speak briefly, the Saviour is from "one thing" and "another" (ἄλλο καὶ ἄλλο). It is true that the invisible and the visible are not the same, as well as that which is outside time and that which is subject to time. However, the Saviour is not "one" and "another" (ἄλλος καὶ ἄλλος). Not at all!" (Gregory of Nazianzus, *Ep. I ad Cledonium*, 20 [SCh 208, 44; PG 37, 180 A]).

20

communicating in the "human" way, also in order to enter into a relationship with God. How can the sacramental signs or sacred words of Scripture be more than mere human creations and contain the presence of *God himself*? In order for there to be true communication, it is not enough to send out a message; reception is needed. If God the Father had spoken to us in Jesus Christ and no one had listened to his message (faith), communication between God and humanity would not have taken place. However, according to the New Testament testimony, whoever enters into relationship with the man Jesus relates to *God himself*, to the Word incarnate. It is the Holy Spirit who works in such a way that the *Word* of God, enclosed in the limitation of the humanity of Jesus, is perceived by believers as the Word *of God*. Gregory of Nazianzus formulates this reality thus: "From the light that is the Father, we understand the Son in the light, this is in the Holy Spirit". And he adds: "brief and simple theology of the Trinity."[13]

18. [*Faith as a Dialogical Reception of Sacramental Revelation*]. Thus, not only does the inseparability of Jesus's humanity with the Word of God come into play, but also the reception by believers (faith) of this Word as divine through the intervention of the Holy Spirit. Herein lies the sacramental logic, through which *God himself* gives himself in the sacraments. The primary sacramentality of Jesus Christ that derived from the Church and that of the seven sacraments are founded on the Trinitarian faith. Only if Jesus Christ is true God can he reveal to us the face of God. But in that case, sacramental communion with Jesus Christ is sacramental communion with God. If the Holy Spirit is true God, then he can open us to God and introduce us into the divine life through the sacramental signs.[14]

19. [*Deployment of Sacramentality*]. Since revelation happens in a sacramental way, the sacramental element must permeate all

---

[13] Gregory Nazianzus, Or. Theol. V (PG 36, 135 C [Or. 31, 3 (SCh 250, 280)]).

[14] Cf. *Catechism of the Catholic Church*, 1091.

believing existence and faith itself. In fact, the sacramentality of revelation, of grace and of the Church is followed by the sacramentality of faith, as a welcome and response to this revelation (DV 5). Faith is generated, cultivated, grows and expresses itself in sacramentality, in that encounter with the living God through the means by which he gives himself. Thus, *sacramentality is the home of faith*. But in this dynamic *faith also manifests itself as the door* (cf. *Acts* 14:27) *of access to the sacramental*: to the encounter and relationship with the Christian God in creation, in history, in the Church, in Scripture,[15] in the sacraments. Without faith, the symbols of a sacramental nature do not actualise their meaning, but they are muted. Sacramentality implies personal communication and communion between God and the believer through the Church and sacramental mediations.

20. [*Correlation of Sacramentality with Anthropology*]. The human person is an incarnate spirit.[16] We human beings are neither mere inanimate matter nor an angelic incorporeal spirit. What most authentically defines us is that complementary union between the material-corporeal, visible, and the spiritual-incorporeal, which is not detached from the material and is made known through it. The case of the personal face, which is the expression of a material body, magnificently manifests this union between our material being, the face, and our spiritual reality, state of mind and personal identification. The face expresses the whole person. The sacramental structure of divine revelation keeps in mind our most authentic reality.[17] It suits our most radical being, our capacity and our way of interrelating in the deepest dimensions of communication. The deepest encounters between human persons are always interpersonal in nature. The encounter with God participates in this nature: it is a personal

---

[15] Cf. Benedict XVI, Apostolic Exhortation *Verbum Domini* (30th September 2010) 56: AAS 102 (2010), 735-736.

[16] Cf. Fourth Lateran Council, *Profession of Faith. Chapter 1: On the Catholic Faith* (DH 800); Vatican II, Pastoral Constitution *Gaudium et spes*, 14.

[17] Cf. Ambrose, *In Lucam II*, 79 (PL 15, 1581); St Thomas Aquinas, *ST* III, q. 61, a. 1.

encounter *with the Trinitarian God* who makes himself present in Scripture, in the Church, and in the sacramental signs.

21. [*Sacramentality of Faith*]. The "sacramentality of faith" basically repeats what has already been said about the Christian faith, because all Christian faith is sacramental faith thanks to the mediation of the Church as we make our pilgrimage to the heavenly homeland. Faith is the reception and response to God's sacramental revelation; and faith expresses itself and nourishes itself in a sacramental way, not being able not to do so in order to be a true Christian faith. From this perspective, the *sacraments* are basically understood as an *act of ecclesial faith. The faith of the Church precedes, generates, sustains and nourishes that of the Christian.* Faith, for its part, is not alien to the sacramental, but is constituted in its very essence by a sacramental impregnation and logic. Therefore, in the relationship between faith and sacraments, two elements come into play which are intimately reciprocal: the sacraments, which presuppose and nourish personal and ecclesial faith; and the necessary sacramental expression of faith. The sacraments, therefore, are configured as a kind of *anamnestic representation that updates and makes the faith visible.*

b) Sacramentality of Creation and History

22. [*God the Creator*]. According to the biblical witness, creation (e.g. *Gn* 1-2) is the first step of the divine economy. Christian understanding holds the free character of creation. God does not create out of necessity or lack of something, if it were so, he would not be God in truth; but because of the overflowing fulness of love that he himself is, in order to distribute its benefits to beings capable of receiving them and responding from the loving logic that presides over creation itself.[18]

---

[18] Theophilus of Antioch, *Aut.* II, 10, 1 (PG 6, 1064; FuP 16, 116); Irenaeus of Lyon, *Adv. Haer.* IV, 14,1; IV, 20, 4 (SCh 100/2, 538; 636); John Duns Scotus, *Ord.* III, d. 32, q. un., n. 21 (Vat. X, 136-137); *Catechism of the Catholic Church*, 293.

23. [*Sacramentality of Creation*]. The Father realises the creative design through the Word and the Spirit. For this reason, creation itself contains the trace of having been shaped by the Word and being directed by the Spirit towards its completion in the same God. As God shapes his mark on creation, theology speaks of a certain "sacramentality of creation", in an analogical sense, inasmuch as, in itself, in its own constitutive creatural being, there is a reference to its Creator (cf. *Wis* 13:1-9; *Rom* 1:19-20; *Acts* 14:15-17; 17:27-28), which allows it to be later elevated and consummated in the redemptive work without any forced extrinsic imposition. In this sense it has been spoken of the book of nature.[19]

24. [*Human Person: responds to God*]. Within visible creation, the human person stands out for having been created in the image and likeness of God (*Gn* 1:26). St Paul underlines the Christological dimension of this image: it is Christ who is the image of the invisible God (*Col* 1:15; *2 Cor* 4:4), since the first Adam was the figure of the one who was to come (cf. *Rom* 5:14). This makes the human person a being in whom God's self-giving in creation can find a personal and free response. For in the image of God, the human person also more intensely realises his own being (identity) the more he gives himself in a relationship of love (otherness).

25. The rich reality of the human person as *imago Dei* includes various aspects, in which, through divine likeness, the capacity to respond to God is highlighted, assimilating his being to the divine.[20] Among them, communion and service stand out.[21] If the Trinitarian God is essentially communion and interpersonal

---

[19] For example: Hugh of Saint Victor, *De tribus diebus*, IV (PL 175, 814 B; CCCM 177, 9); Richard of Saint Victor, *De Trin*. I, 9; Bonaventure, *Itinerarium*, I, 14; Benedict XVI, Apostolic Exhortation *Verbum Domini* (30th September 2010) 7: AAS 102 (2010), 688.

[20] Ephrem, *Hymni de Fide*, 18: 4-5 (CSCO 154, 70 ; 155, 54).

[21] Cf. International Theological Commission, *Communion and Stewardship: The Human Person Created in the Image of God* [2004]. See also our § 20.

relationship, the human person, as the image of God, has been created to live in communion and interpersonal relationship. This is magnificently expressed in the sexual difference: "God created man in his own image, in the image of God he created him, male and female he created them" (*Gn* 1:27). Hence the human person attains his own being insofar as he unfolds his relationality and his capacity for communion: with other human beings, with creation and with God. In Jesus Christ the exercise of this dynamic of communion and relationship shines forth in its fulness. The filial life which is shown in him manifests the height of the human vocation (cf. GS 10, 22, 41).

26. As a relational being and created for communion the human person can be defined by language. Now, language is a reality of symbolic order, which points, on the one hand, to the expression of what reality is of its own (God's creation), and, on the other, to interpersonal communication (communion). As a symbolic being, created in the image of God, the person attains his most authentic reality insofar as he inscribes the realisation of his being in a specific sphere of symbolic expression, in which all the richness of his own being is unfolded: as a creatural being, as an interpersonal being and as a being called to communion with God. The sacraments faithfully and efficiently gather,express, develop and strengthen this rich framework.

27. As an eloquent sign of his dignity and friendship with God, man is also charged with exercising delegated government over creation (*Gn* 2:15; cf. 1:28; *Wis* 9:2), naming all other creatures (*Gn* 2:19-20) and taking care of them according to God's plan.[22] For this reason, human activity in the world is directed towards the glorification of God, recognising in it the mark of the Creator (cf. GS 34). In this way, the human person leads creation through a kind of "cosmic priesthood" towards its true purpose: the manifestation of the glory of God.

---

[22] Cf. Pope Francis, Encyclical Letter *Laudato si* (24th May 2015) esp. 106-114: AAS 107 (2015), 872-877.

28. [*Sacramentality of History*]. God's desire to communicate his gifts is not restricted to leaving the imprint of his love in creation. The story of the people of Israel as a whole can be properly viewed as a story of God's love for his people. Within this history some special events stand out that prefigure essential aspects, which found the sacramental relationship of God with his people, which will reach its culmination with Christ. In all of them there is a visible perceptibility of the way God relates to his people, gracing them. Thus, a sort of first grammar for the later constitution of the sacramental language *sensu stricto* is discovered in them. Among these events, of which we can make a sacramental reading, are found: the choice of Abraham, of David and the Israelites, and the gift of the Law, which will become the basis of every sacramental discourse; the many covenants, within the one divine design, in which a new relationship is established between God and humanity, and in which sacramentality is at work in a special way; the liberation of Israel from Egypt, the exile and the return to Jerusalem, in which the future salvation of Christ is anticipated in a new way, as the sacramental function of the Church is represented in figure (*typos*); the presence of God in the midst of his people in the Tabernacle and in the Temple, which will acquire a particular density in Christ and the Christian sacraments. Israel will remember and actualise liturgically this density of God's presence through different cultic rites (e.g. sacrifices), sacred signs (e.g. circumcision), and feasts (e.g. Passover), always illuminated by the reading of the Word. Christian theology designates these realities as sacraments of the Old Law and attributes to them a salvific character by their reference to Christ[23] and in proportion to the faith of those who celebrated them (*ex opere operantis*). Therefore, it is discovered that salvation history itself possesses a certain sacramental

---

[23] "Proinde prima sacramenta, quae observabantur et celebrabantur ex Lege, praenuntiativa erant Christi venturi: quae cum suo adventu Christus implevisset, ablata sunt; et ideo ablata, quia impleta; non enim venit solvere Legem sed adimplere" (Augustine, *Contra Faustum*, XIX, 13; PL 42, 355).

nature.[24] Through historical events, signs and words, closely linked, God himself comes close to his people and communicates to them his will, his love, his predilection, at the same time as he shows them the way of friendship with God and the truest human life.

29. [*Sin*]. Throughout history, many believers of all times have lived in friendship with God, accepting his gift and responding generously to God's mercy and faithfulness. However, it is also true that, despite God's insistence, men do not always accept this offer of love. From the beginning, not only is there the temptation to ignore the path of friendship with God, as the best means of realising what it means to be a human person, but his offer is also rejected (*Gn* 3). The history of Israel, and that of humanity, can be understood as an eager search for God to conquer again the cordial friendship with man when it has been lost (e.g. *Ez* 16). From this we can understand the profound sense that many of the cultural signs of the Old Testament salvific order contain a meaning of expiation or reconciliation with God (e.g. ablutions, sacrifices).

c) The Incarnation:
Centre, Summit, and Key to the Sacramental Economy

30. [*Jesus Christ: Ur-Sacrament*]. God's desire to give himself acquires its unsurpassable summit in Jesus Christ (cf. DV 2). By virtue of this hypostatic union (cf. DH 301-302), the humanity of Christ, true man, "in all things like unto us, save in sin" (*Heb* 4:15), is the humanity of the Son of God, of the eternal Word incarnate "for us and for our salvation" (DH 150). Recent theology affirms that Jesus Christ is the primary sacrament (*Ur-Sacrament*) and the key to the sacramental structure of salvation history. In synthesis, in Jesus Christ we discover that *the* divine *economy* of

---

[24] Irenaeus of Lyon, *Adv. haer.* IV, 21, 3 (SCh 100/2, 684); Tertullian, *De baptismo*, 3 (CCSL 1, 278-279).

salvation, *because it is incarnational, is sacramental.*[25] For this reason it can be truly affirmed that "the sacraments are at the centre of Christianity. The loss of the sacraments is equivalent to the loss of the incarnation and vice versa."[26] For in Jesus Christ, as the summit of history and the fulness of time (*Gal* 4:4), there is the closest possible unity between a creatural symbol, its humanity, and what is symbolised, the saving presence of God in his Son in the midst of history. Christ's humanity, as humanity inseparable from the divine person of the Son of God, is a "real symbol" of the divine person. In this supreme case, the created communicates to the highest degree the presence of God.

31. [*The Humanity of the Glorious Crucified One: Foundation of the Sacraments*]. Consequently, Christ's humanity is intrinsically empowered to be the "mediator and fulness of all revelation" (DV 2), in a way that is qualitatively insurmountable with regard to any other creatural reality, since it is the humanity proper to the Son of God (cf. *Heb* 1:1-2). That to which creation inchoatively pointed is realised in an eminent way in the humanity of Jesus Christ. All the actions and words of Jesus Christ, the eternal Word incarnate, anointed by the Spirit, are qualified by the incarnation. In such a way that through his words and deeds, and the manifestation of his whole person, he transmits to us the revelation of God (cf. DV 4). Thus Jesus Christ himself is the mystery of God transmitted and revealed to men (cf. *Col* 2:2-3; 1:27; 4:3), present in the various salvific mysteries of his life: birth, baptism, transfiguration, etc. Now the unfolding of the mystery of Christ reaches its summit in the glorious death and resurrection, to which the gift of the Spirit continues (cf. DV 4). There the revelation of God's love to the end (cf. *Jn* 13:1) and its redeeming power are condensed with a sublime

---

[25] "Caro salutis est cardo" (Tertullian, *De resurrectione*, 8; CCSL 2, 931). Cf. Congregation for the Doctrine of the Faith, Letter *Placuit Deo* (22nd February 2018) 1-2, 4, 8 (incarnational) in correlation with 13-14 (sacramental).

[26] Joseph Ratzinger, "Prefazione," in H. Luthe (ed.), *Incontrare Cristo nei sacramenti*, (Milano, 1988), 8.

and insurmountable intensity. The result is the forgiveness of sin (cf. *Col* 2:13-14) and the openness to participate in the eternal life of the Risen One, through the gift of the Spirit who makes us sharers in the divine nature (cf. *2 Pt* 1:4). Thus we understand that Jesus Christ concentrates the foundation and the source of all sacramentality, which then unfolds in the different sacramental signs that generate the Church, where there are gathered unique aspects and dense moments of his life: forgiveness of sins (Penance), healing of the sick (Anointing of the Sick), death and resurrection (Baptism and Eucharist), election and institution of disciples as pastors of the community (Orders), and so on. The sacramental logic, inscribed in the Trinitarian revelation, is prolonged and condensed in the sacraments, in which Christ makes himself present in a particularly intense way (SC 7). The sacramental structure and logic of faith hang on Jesus Christ, the Incarnate and redeeming Word.[27]

32. Indeed, Jesus does not simply communicate to us something important about God. He is not simply *a* teacher, *a* messenger, or *a* prophet, but the personal presence of God's Word in creation. Since he as true man is inseparable from God, whom he calls "Father," communion with him means communion with God (*Jn* 10:30; 14:6, 9). The Father wants to lead all men through the Holy Spirit to communion with Jesus Christ. Jesus Christ is, at the same time, the way that leads to life and life itself (*Jn* 14:6); in other words: "He is, at the same time, the Saviour and Salvation."[28] With the sacraments of the Word celebrated in the Spirit, especially with the memorial of his death and resurrection, we are offered a way and a remedy after the loss of sin, to attain communion and personal relationship with God through participation in the life of Christ, inserting ourselves in him. Thus, the work of salvation is accomplished, which completes and culminates its beginning with creation. However, God makes the acceptance of this gift dependent on

---

[27] Thomas Aquinas, *ST* III, q. 60, a. 6 corp.

[28] Congregation for the Doctrine of the Faith, Letter *Placuit Deo* (22nd February 2018) § 11.

the *cooperation* of the recipients. As the case of Our Lady, the ecclesial model of the disciple, shows, grace respects freedom, it is not imposed in a coercive way without the consent of freedom (*Lk* 1:38), even if assent is made possible by grace itself (*Lk* 1:28).

d) The Church and the Sacraments in the Sacramental Economy

33. [*The Church: Grund-Sakrament*]. The historical tangibility of grace, which has historically been made present in Jesus Christ, remains privileged, but derived, through the work of the Holy Spirit in the Church.[29] To the being of the Church belongs a visible and historical structure, at the service of the transmission of invisible grace, which she herself receives from Christ and transmits thanks to the Spirit. There is a remarkable analogy between the Church and the Incarnate Word (cf. LG 8; SC 2).From these premises, contemporary theology has deepened the understanding of the Church as fundamental sacrament (*Grund-Sakrament*), in a line close to the understanding of Vatican II of the Church as the universal sacrament of salvation.[30] As a sacrament, the Church is at the service of the salvation of the world (LG 1; GS 45), at the service of the transmission of grace whose reception has made it a sacrament. Sacramentality always has a missionary character, of service for the good of others.

34. Now, also as a sacrament, in the Church itself there is already a perceptibility of God's grace, of the irruption of the Kingdom of God. Thus, if on the one hand the Church is at the service of the establishment of the Kingdom of God; on the other hand, the presence of the Kingdom of Christ in mystery is already present in her (LG 3). Endowed with these means of grace, she can truly

---

[29] "Moritur Christus ut fiat Ecclesia" (Augustine, *In Johannis Ev.* IX, 10: CCSL, 36, 96; PL 35, 1463).

[30] Cf. Vatican II, Dogmatic Constitution *Lumen gentium*, 1, 9,48, 59; *Sacrosanctum concilium*, 5, 26; Decree *Ad gentes* 1, 5; Pastoral Constitution *Gaudium et spes*, 42, 45.

be the germ and the beginning of the kingdom[31] (LG 5). As a pilgrim and made up of sinners, there is no total identification between the Church and the Kingdom of God; as a reality constituted by grace, it possesses an eschatological dimension, culminating in the heavenly Church and the communion of saints[32] (cf. LG 48-49).

35. [*The Church: Christological and Pneumatological Reality*]. As creatures who abide in the Trinity, that is, "the people united within the unity of the Father, of the Son and of the Holy Spirit,"[33] the Church not only maintains an intimate relationship with the Incarnate Word, to the point of being able to affirm with truth that it is the Body of Christ (cf. LG 7), but also with the Holy Spirit. And this is the case not only because the Spirit, the great gift of the Risen One (cf. *Jn* 7:39; 14:26; 15:26; 20:22), works in her constitution (cf. LG 4), dwells in her and in the faithful as in a temple (*1 Cor* 3:16; 6:19), unifies it and generates the missionary dynamism inherent in it (cf. *Acts* 2:4-13); but also because the Church is a spiritual, pneumatic people (cf. LG 12), enriched by the various gifts that the Spirit gives to the faithful for the good of the whole community (cf. *Rom* 12:4-8; *1 Cor* 12:12-30; *1 Pt* 4:10). These charismatic gifts lead to a particular appropriation of the richness of the Word of God and of sacramental grace, strengthening the community and promoting its mission (cf. AA 3), in short: strengthening the sacramentality of the Church.[34]

36. [*Sacramental Continuity of the Salvific Order*]. The salvation that was historically offered in Jesus Christ continues in the

---

[31] Cf. St John Paul II, Encyclical Letter *Redemptoris missio* (7th December 1990) 18: AAS 83 (1991), 265-266; Congregation for the Doctrine of the Faith, Declaration *Dominus Iesus* (6th August 2000) 18: AAS 92 (2000), 759-760.

[32] Cf. International Theological Commission, *Select Themes of Ecclesiology* [1982], chap. 10: "The Eschatological Character of the Church: Kingdom and Church."

[33] Vatican II, Dogmatic Constitution *Lumen gentium*, 4, with internal citation of Cyprian, *De Dominica oratione*, 23 (PL 4, 553; CSEL 3/I, 285).

[34] Cf. Congregation for the Doctrine of the Faith, Letter *Iuvenescit Ecclesia* (15th May 2016), § 23; see also §§ 11 and 13.

Church (cf. *Lk* 10:16), the Body of Christ, through life-giving sacraments, thanks to the action of the Spirit[35]; "what was visible in Christ has passed into the sacraments" of the Church.[36] The Catholic Church holds that the seven sacraments have been instituted by Christ,[37] since only he can authoritatively unite effectively the gift of his saving grace to certain signs.[38] This affirmation emphasises that the sacraments are not an ecclesial creation, and the Church cannot change their substance,[39] but that they are based on the event Christ took as a whole: Incarnation, Life, Death and Resurrection. The institution of the sacraments gathers meaning from the Incarnation and proclaims it (cf. §§ 30-32), for they specify characteristics of Jesus's humanity, the unfolding of the mysteries of his human life which culminate in Easter, for here Jesus gives himself fully as the source of all graces, beginning with the gift of the Spirit. The Church is enlightened by the Spirit which she received at Pentecost and is encouraged by the celebration of the Eucharist (cf. PO 5), which is the source and summit of the Christian life (SC 10; LG 11). The Church has recognised that the sacramental gift of Christ is eminently continued in the seven sacramental signs which go back to the same Christ in different ways,[40] while maintaining that divine grace is not limited exclusively to the seven sacraments.[41]

---

[35] Cf. *Catechism of the Catholic Church*, 1116.

[36] Leo the Great, *Sermo* 74, 2 (PL 54, 398). Cf. Ambrose of Milan, *Apol. pro Prophetae David*, XII, 58 (PL 16, 875); *Catechism of the Catholic Church*, 1115.

[37] Cf. Council of Trent, Session 7, "Canons concerning the Sacraments," canon 1 (DH 1601); *Catechism of the Catholic Church*, 1114.

[38] Cf. Thomas Aquinas, *ST* III, q. 64, a.2.

[39] Clement VI, Letter *Super quibusdam* of 1351 (DH 1061) ; Council of Trent, Session 21, "Doctrine and Canons on Communion under both Species and Communion of Little Children, chap. 2 (DH 1728); Pius X, Letter *Ex quo, nono* of 1910 (DH 3556); Pius XII, Apostolic Constitution *Sacramentum ordinis* of 1947 (DH 3857).

[40] See below for each of the sacraments that we deal with the brief note on scriptural foundation that we offer.

[41] Thomas Aquinas, *ST* III, q. 64, a. 2, ad 3.

37. [*Sacramental Grace and non-Christians*]. The Church affirms that the grace that justifies and gives salvation is given and, therefore, true faith is also given outside the visible Church, but not independently of Jesus (primordial sacrament) and the church (fundamental sacrament). The action of the Holy Spirit is not limited to the limits of the visible Church, but "its presence and action are universal, without any limit of space or time."[42] Non-Christian religions may contain aspects of truth and may be the means and indirect signs of the spiritual grace of Jesus Christ. But this does not mean that they are salvific paths parallel to Christ or independent of Christ and his Church.[43]

38. [*Sacramental Grace and Faith*]. In short, the Word of God, creative and effective, has created the interpersonal language of the sacramental words, which are the sacraments; words in which the Word continues to act thanks to the Spirit. In the words that the minister pronounces in the name of the Church, e.g. "I baptise you", the Risen Christ continues to speak and act.[44] Since the sacraments make possible today by the Spirit a personal relationship with the dead and risen Lord, they have no meaning without such a relationship, which is condensed in the word "faith."

39. [*Sacraments: Supreme Exercise of Ecclesial Sacramentality*]. The fundamental sacramentality of the Church is exercised in a privileged way and with special intensity in the celebration of the sacraments. The sacraments always have an ecclesial nature: in them the Church puts her own being at stake, at the service of the transmission of the saving grace of the risen Christ, through

---

[42] St John Paul II, Encyclical Letter *Redemptoris missio* (7th December 1990) 28: AAS 83 (1991), 273. Cf. St John Paul II, Encyclical Letter *Dominum et Vivificantem* (18th May 1986) 53: AAS 78 (1986), 874-875; Vatican II, Pastoral Constitution *Gaudium et spes*, 22.

[43] Cf. St John Paul II, Encyclical Letter *Redemptoris missio* (7th December 1990) 28-29: AAS 83 (1991), 273-275; International Theological Commission, *Christianity and the World Religions* [1996], §§ 81-87.

[44] Cf. Augustine, *In Johannis ev.*, V, 18 (CCSL 36, 51-53; PL 35, 1424); John Chrysostom, *In 2 Tm. Hom.*, 2, 4 (PG 62, 612).

the assistance of the Spirit. Therefore, each and every sacrament is an intrinsically ecclesial act. According to the Fathers, the sacraments are always celebrated in the faith of the Church, since they have been entrusted to the Church. In each and every sacrament, the faith of the Church precedes the faith of the singular faithful. It is, in fact, a personal exercise of the ecclesial faith. Therefore, without participation in the ecclesial faith, such symbolic acts become mute, inasmuch as faith opens the door to the operative sacramental signification.

40. [*Sacramentals*]. Ecclesial sacramentality is not only embodied in the sacraments. There is another series of sacramental realities that form part of the life and faith of the Church, among which Sacred Scripture stands out. For Christian piety, of great importance are the so-called sacramentals, which are sacred signs, created according to the model of the sacraments. Sacramentals dispose towards the sacraments and sanctify the various circumstances of life (SC 60). What is proper to the sacraments is that in them there is an authorised and sure ecclesial commitment to the transmission of the grace of Christ, provided that all the requirements are fulfilled. In the sacramentals, however, one cannot speak of an efficacy similar to that of the sacraments.[45] In them, there is a preparation for the reception of grace and a disposition to cooperate with it, not an efficacy *ex opere operato* (cf. § 65), exclusive of the sacraments. Thus, while the water of baptism produces the effect of forgiveness of sins in the womb of the sacramental celebration, holy water, remembrance of baptism, does not cause an effect by itself, but in the measure in which it is received with faith, for example when crossing oneself at the entrance to the temple.

---

[45] *Catechism of the Catholic Church*, 1670. Cf. Vatican II, Constitution on the Sacred Liturgy, *Sacrosanctum concilium*, 61.

e) The Axes of the Sacramental Economy

41. Systematising the main results of our journey, we can establish the following fundamental points:

a) The divine Trinitarian economy, because it is incarnational, is sacramental. Since the economy is sacramental in nature, the seven sacraments instituted by Christ, guarded and celebrated by the Church, are of capital importance within the Church.

b) The sacramentality of the divine economy refers to faith. It is through faith that this sacramentality is grasped and inhabited. The perception of sacramentality through faith is closely linked to: the Incarnation, through which the divine plan is made visible in a historical and tangible way; the Holy Spirit, who perpetuates the gifts of Christ by transmitting saving grace through sacramental symbols; the Church, a visible and historical institution which, having received the sacramental gifts, continues to celebrate them in order to nourish and strengthen the faith of the faithful.

c) Jesus Christ instituted the sacraments and gave them to his Church so that the mysteries of faith would be represented in a visible way. The believer who participates in these mysteries receives the gifts that are represented in them. Consequently, the transmission of faith implies not only the communication of doctrinal contents of an intellectual character, but also, and together with them, the existential insertion into the frame of the sacramental economy, which the encyclical *Lumen fidei* has masterfully described:

"But what is communicated in the Church, what is handed down in her living Tradition, is the new light born of an encounter with the living God, a light that touches us at the core of our being and engages our minds, wills and emotions, opening us to relationships lived in communion with God and with others. There is a special means for

35

passing down this fulness, a means capable of engaging the entire person, body and spirit, interior life and relationship with others. It is the sacraments, celebrated in the Church's liturgy. They communicate an incarnate memory, linked to the times and places of our lives, linked to all our senses; in them the whole person is engaged as a member of a living subject and part of a network of communitarian relationships. While the sacraments are indeed sacraments of faith [cf. SC 59], it can also be said that faith itself possesses a sacramental structure. The awakening of faith is linked to the dawning of a new sacramental sense of the life of man and of Christian existence, in which visible and material is open to the mystery of the eternal."[46]

d) The structuring of the sacramental economy is dialogical. Faith represents the moment of the graceful response of the human person to the gift of God. There is an essential reciprocity between faith and sacramentality, in a general way, and between faith and sacraments, in a specific way.

e) The dialogical nature (faith) of the economy implies a series of significant consequences when it comes to understanding theologically and pastorally offering each of the different sacraments. From the previous statements, it can be argued with good foundation that effective sacraments without faith would suppose a mere causal mechanism. Without faith, it would suppose something alien to the realm of the relations between the Trinitarian God and men, which are of a dialogical and interpersonal nature. Effective sacraments without faith would also suppose an action of a magical type, alien to the Christian faith and to the sacramental logic of the economy; it would also suppose a conception of God, incompatible with Catholic doctrine, which does not take into account that the same divine gift contains the grace which enables the creature

---

[46] Francis, Encyclical Letter *Lumen fidei* (29th June 2013) 40 : AAS 105 (2013), 582.

to consent and collaborate with divine action in the measure proper to the creature. In other words: *since the Trinitarian economy as sacramental is dialogical, it is not possible to understand the action of grace that is given in them according to the model of a kind of sacramental automatism.*

2.2. THE RECIPROCITY BETWEEN FAITH AND THE SACRAMENTS OF FAITH

a) Lights from the path of faith of the disciples

42. [*Growth of Faith*]. Peter, as spokesman for the disciples, in response to Jesus's question, formulates a confession of faith: "You are the Christ" (*Mk* 8:29 and par.). However, Peter had to mature this initial faith because when Jesus begins to explain that he is a Messiah after the manner of the suffering Son of Man, a Messiah who will be crucified, Peter rejects him and Jesus harshly reproaches him (*Mk* 8:31-33). Thus, Peter had to realise a path of growth in faith, combining his unconditional adherence to Jesus as Christ with the knowledge of the doctrinal aspects that this adherence implied. This not only concerns Peter, but reflects the reality of each believer. The apostles themselves show us the way with their petition to the Lord; "Increase our faith" (*Lk* 17:5). Paul warns about this gradual growth and counts on it, since it refers to "the measure of faith which God has given to each one" (*Rom* 12:3; cf. 12:6). He also admonishes the Christians of Corinth, whom he is to treat as "children in Christ," giving them "milk" instead of solid food (cf. *1 Cor* 3:1-2). The letter to the Hebrews echoes this difference by speaking to members of the Christian community (cf. *Heb* 5:11-14). Going beyond the basic rudiments of Christian doctrine and faith, solid food is directed to believers who in their Christian lives exercise discernment of good and evil, to those whose entire existence is illuminated by the light of faith.[47]

---

[47] Francis, Encyclical Letter *Lumen fidei* (29th June 2013) 4 : AAS 105 (2013), 557.

43. The disciples and other admirers of Jesus, the crowd, captured something special in the figure of Jesus before Passover. In particular, in the context of healings we are told of a "faith." The phenomenology we find is quite varied: Jesus performs miracles without express mention of faith (e.g. *Mk* 1:14-45; 3:1-6; 6:33-44); thanks to the faith of petitioners who intercede on behalf of another person (*Mk* 2:5; *Lk* 7:28-29); in spite of a faith that considers itself scarce (*Mk* 9:24); or precisely, thanks to faith (*Mk* 5:34). The disciples are encouraged in many ways to grow in faith (*Mt* 6:30; 8:26; 14:31; 16:8; 17:20), in faith in God and in his power (*Mk* 12:24) and in understanding the unique position of Jesus in God's plan (*Jn* 14:1).

44. The death of Jesus put this initial adhesion of the disciples to the test. They all dispersed and fled (*Mk* 14:50). The women who went to the tomb very early in the morning intended to anoint the corpse (*Mk* 16:1-2). However, with the novelty of the resurrection and the gift of the promised Spirit (*Jn* 14:16-17, 26), the faith of the disciples is strengthened, to the point that they will be able to initiate others and strengthen them in their faith (*Jn* 21:15-18; *Lk* 22:32). Pentecost marks the pinnacle of the disciples' journey of faith. Not only do they fully adhere to Jesus, dead and risen, as the Lord and Son of the living God, but they become bold witnesses, full of parrhesia, able to speak of God's deeds and transmit faith in all languages thanks to the Spirit. Now they will be witnesses, even martyrs, proclaiming Jesus as the crucified and risen Messiah, Son of the living God, Lord of the living and the dead. In this figure of faith, the believing adherence to Jesus includes the doctrinal content of the resurrection and the unfolding of its meaning. According to the sources, this passage to faith in the resurrection was neither easy nor automatic, particularly for those who, like us, did not benefit from an apparition of the Risen One (Thomas: *Jn* 20:24-29). The pericope of Emmaus (*Lk* 24:13-35) provides some valuable clues for initiating others on the path of faith.[48] Walk at

---

[48] Cf. XV Ordinary Assembly of the Synod of Bishops on *Young People, Faith and Vocational Discernment. Final Document, passim and spec.* §4

the pace of those who, although disappointed, express some concern. Listen to their concerns and welcome them. Confront them patiently with the light of salvation history reflected in Scripture, stimulating the desire to know more and better the plan of God. This opens the way to a faith that matures in the sacramental and ecclesial dimensions proper to faith.

45. [*Need to Discern with Patience*]. The Bible, a reflection of salvation history, presents a multitude of situations in which faith, as a dynamic and vital reality with advances and setbacks, finds itself in multiple positions, from the search for a tangible benefit, which looks exclusively at personal interest, to the extreme generosity of confessional love. Jesus categorically rejected hypocrisy (e.g., *Mk* 8:15), called for conversion and belief in the Gospel (*Mk* 1:15), but he magnanimously welcomed many who came to him longing in some way for God's salvation. For this reason, one must appreciate the value of incipient faith, the faith that is on its way to maturity, the faith that in its desire to know God does not exclude unresolved questions and hesitations, the imperfect faith that finds some difficulty in adhering to the totality of the contents that the Church holds as revealed. It is the task of all pastoral agents to help in the growth of faith, whatever its stage, so that it may discover the whole face of Christ and the record of doctrinal elements which includes the believing adhesion to the dead and risen Lord. Because of this diversity, the same faith is not required for all sacraments or in the same circumstances of life.

b) Modulations of Faith

46. [*Need for Some Clarifications*]. Classical reflection on faith and sacraments has highlighted the articulation both of the irrevocability of the gift of Christ (*ex opere operato*) and of the necessary dispositions for a valid and fruitful reception of the sacraments. These provisions are misunderstood at their roots if they are seen as a sort of arbitrarily imposed hindrance to impede or make more difficult access to the sacraments. Nor do they have anything to do with "elitism," which would despise

the faith of the simple. It is simply a matter of highlighting the interior dispositions of the believer to receive what Christ freely wants to give us in the sacraments. That is to say, what is manifested in these dispositions is the adequate adjustment between faith and the sacraments of faith: what faith by its very nature do the sacraments of faith ask for? Without losing the gains acquired during the course of theological reflection, it is convenient to expound on some of the various aspects of personal faith, and then discern in the following chapters how they come into play in the sacramental celebration understood as a dialogical encounter.

47. [*Theological Dimension*]. The peculiarity of faith lies in the fact that it is expressly inscribed in the relationship with God. Theology distinguishes different aspects within the one act of faith.[49] This is the difference between "credere Deum," believing in God, which refers to the cognitive element of faith, to what is believed (*fides quae*). The proper thing about faith is to be directed towards God. That is why faith has a *theo*-centric character. "Credere Deo," to believe in God, expresses the formal aspect, the reason for giving assent. God is also the cause by which one believes (*fides qua*), so faith has a *theo*-logical character. Thus, God is the object believed and the reason for faith. With these fundamental aspects, however, the act of faith is not reflected in its integrity. There is also "credere in Deum," believing towards God. Here the volitional aspect is more clearly manifested, inasmuch as integrating the two previous moments; faith also includes a desire and a movement towards God, the beginning of a journey towards God, which will be consummated in the eschatological encounter with him in eternal life. For this reason, faith has a *theo*-eschatological dimension. The act of faith in its entirety presupposes the concurrence of the three aspects. This occurs in a characteristic way in the "in Deum," which includes the other two.

---

[49] E.g., Augustine, *De symb.* I, 181 (PL 40, 1190-1191) ; Peter Lombard, *Summa Sententiarum*, III. d. 23, c. 2-4 (PL 192, 805-806); Thomas Aquinas, *ST* II-II, q. 2, a.2.

48. [*Trinitarian Dimension*]. In Christian faith, believing in God implies believing in Jesus Christ as the Son, thanks to the Spirit. Characteristically, the symbol repeats three times "in Deum," referring to each of the divine persons, marking the Trinitarian dimension. The formulation refers to the difference from any other act of comparable trust, for example, in a human person.[50] The relationship with the Trinitarian God is distinguished from the relationship with that which has been produced or created by him. *In Deum credere* represents the perfect figure of personal relationship; it includes hope and love,[51] or as Augustine describes it: "to adhere by believing God, him who does good, in order to do good by cooperating with him."[52] This is the true form of faith, which includes the two dimensions already mentioned: believing in God and believing God (*credere Deum* and *credere Deo*) .[53] The formula "credo in Deum" is not reduced to expressing a confession and a conviction, but the process of conversion and surrender, the way of faith of the believer. It is precisely this personal dimension that endows the symbol and its various articles with coherence. This occurs especially intensely in sacramental celebrations, proper to the economy of the Spirit,[54] in which it is perceived that faith is always ecclesial[55]:

---

[50] Paschasius Radbertus, *De fide, spe et car.* I, 6 no. 1 (PL 120, 1402 ff.).

[51] Faustus of Riez, *De spir. S.* I, 1 (CSEL 21, 103).

[52] "Credendo adhaerere ad bene cooperandum bona cooperanti Deo" (*Enarr. in Ps.* 77:8; CCSL 39, 1073).

[53] Augustine, *In Iohannis ev.*, XXIX, 6 (CCSL 36, 287; PL 35, 1684): "Ut credatis in eum, not ut credatis ei. Sed si creditis in eum, creditis ei, non autem continuo, qui credit ei credit in eum..." Also Thomas Aquinas, *ST* II-II, q. 2, a.2.

[54] "The Church was made manifest to the world on the day of Pentecost by the outpouring of the Holy Spirit (cf. SC 6; LG 2). The gift of the Spirit ushers in a new era in the 'dispensation of the mystery' the age of the Church, during which Christ manifests, makes present, and communicates his work of salvation through the Liturgy of his Church, 'until he comes' (*1 Cor* 11:26). During this age of the Church, Christ now lives and acts in and with his Church, in a new way appropriate to this new age. He acts through the sacraments in what the common Tradition of the East and the West calls "the sacramental economy," this consists in the communication (or 'dispensation') of the fruits of Christ's Paschal mystery in the celebration of the Church's 'sacramental' liturgy" (*Catechism of the Catholic Church*, 1076).

[55] Thomas Aquinas, *ST* II-II, q. 1, a.9, ad 3: "confessio fidei traditur in symbolo quasi ex persona totius Ecclesiae, quae per fidem unitur."

In the celebration of the sacraments, the Church hands down her memory especially through the profession of faith. The creed does not only involve giving one's assent to a body of abstract truths; rather, when it is recited the whole life is drawn into a journey towards full communion with the living God. We can say that in the creed believers are invited to enter into the mystery which they profess and to be transformed by it.[56]

49. In the Trinitarian faith there is implied a personal relationship of the believer with each one of the persons of the Holy Trinity. By faith, the Spirit leads us to the knowledge of the whole truth (*Jn* 16:12-13). No one can confess Jesus as Lord except in the Spirit (*1 Cor* 12:3). Thus, the Spirit dwells in the believer and empowers him to walk in the Spirit towards God, to bear witness to his faith, to spread Christian charity, to live in hope, to reach the maturity of the fulness of the believer, to the measure of Christ (cf. *Eph* 4:13). Therefore, the Spirit acts in the believer both in the subjective act of believing itself, as well as in the contents believed and, of course, in the vital dynamism that it imprints on the believer. This dynamism implies a deeper appropriation of the Beatitudes, a portrait of the heart of Christ and, therefore, of the disciple.[57] With his gifts, the Spirit strengthens the individual believer[58] and the Church. By faith we confess Jesus Christ as the Lord, the Son of the living God; we become his disciples, walking towards conformity with him (cf. *Rom* 8:29). Through faith, and thanks to the mediation of the Son and the Spirit, we know the plan of God the Father, we enter into relationship with him, we praise him, we bless him and we obey him as beloved children. We set out to fulfil his will for us, for history and for creation.

---

[56] Francis, Encyclical Letter *Lumen fidei* (29th June 2013) 45: AAS 105 (2013), 585.

[57] Cf. Francis, Apostolic Exhortation *Gaudete et exsultate* (19th March 2018) 65-94.

[58] Cf. *Catechism of the Catholic Church*, 1830-1832.

50. [*The Reformation and its Influence*]. The Reformation has exerted an influence that is hardly overestimated on the supremacy of the individual act of faith over the confession of ecclesial faith. The singular characteristics that stand out are the concentration of faith in one's own justification, the qualification of the act of faith as an appropriation of grace, and the identification of the certainty of faith with the certainty of salvation. This trending subjectivisation of truth has also influenced part of the theology of faith in recent Catholicism, when it, under the umbrella of personalism, has taken on a unilateral subjectivist orientation. For this reason, in these approaches faith is described less as confession than as a personal relationship of trust (faith in someone), and, at least tendentially, is opposed to doctrinal faith (faith in something).

51. [*Fides qua: fides quae*]. If the dialogue of God with man involves a sacramental nature, which crosses the whole of revelation, then the response, through faith, will also have to take on a sacramental logic, impelled and made possible by the Spirit. There can be no subjective understanding of faith alone (*fides qua*), which is not linked to the authentic truth of God (*fides quae*), handed down in revelation and preserved in the Church. There is therefore "a profound unity between the act by which we believe and the contents to which we give our assent. The apostle Paul helps us to enter into this reality when he writes: 'one believes with the heart and one confesses with the mouth' (cf. *Rom* 10:10)."[59] It is the sacramental signs of God's presence in the world and history that inspire, express and preserve faith. In the Christian conception it is not possible to think of a faith without sacramental expression (in the face of subjectivist privatisation), nor a sacramental practise in the absence of ecclesial faith (against ritualism). Where faith excludes identification with confession and the life of the Church, this faith is no longer an integration in Christ. The privatised and disincarnated faith of the Gnostics

---

[59] Benedict XVI, Apostolic Letter issued Motu Proprio *Porta fidei* (11th October 2011) 10: AAS 103 (2011), 728.

runs through the history of Christianity like a temptation.[60] But there is also often the opposite tendency, namely, an outward faith, which adheres verbally to the confession of faith without appropriating it through personal understanding or prayer. Subjectivist privatisation and ritualism mark the two dangers that the Christian faith must overcome at all costs.[61]

52. [*Fundamental equality of all believers in the faith*]. The personal faith of each believer can have varying degrees both with regard to the intensity of the relationship with the Trinitarian God and with regard to the degree to which its contents are made explicit. Faith being a relationship of a personal nature, there inherently belongs to its own dynamics the capacity to grow in both dimensions: in the knowledge and appropriation of the truths of the faith and its internal consistency, on the one hand, and on the confidence and the determination to orient all existence from the intimate relationship with God, on the other hand.[62]

53. In the history of theology, the question of the indispensable minimum has been raised with regard to the reflex knowledge of the content of faith, as well as the role of the so-called "implicit faith." The scholastic theologians showed a great appreciation of the faith of the simple (*simplices, minores*). According to Thomas Aquinas, not everyone should be required to have the same degree of explicitness in terms of knowing how to reflect the contents of faith.[63] The difference between "implicit" and "explicit" faith refers to certain contents of the faith that are either included in the same faith and, in that sense, are

---

[60] Cf. Lately Pope Francis, Apostolic Exhortation, *Gaudete et exsultate*, (19th March 2018) §43; Cf. Congregation for the Doctrine of the Faith, Letter *Placuit Deo* (22nd February 2018) § 12.

[61] Cf. Pope Francis, Apostolic Exhortation, *Gaudete et exsultate*, (19th March 2018) §§ 48-49; Cf. Congregation for the Doctrine of the Faith, Letter *Placuit Deo* (22nd February 2018) §§ 2-3.

[62] Hugh of St Victor, *Sacr.* I pars 10 (PL 176, 327-344), chapters 3 and 4: *De incremento fidei.*

[63] Thomas Aquinas, *De Ver.* 14, a.11, corp. ; *ST* II-II, q.2, a.6.7.8

settled in the act of believing – implicit; or they are believed reliably and consciously (*actu cogitatum credere*) – explicit. It is not necessary that simple believers know how to give a detailed intellectual account of Trinitarian or soteriological developments. Implicit faith in itself includes the fundamental predisposition to identify with the faith of the Church and to unite oneself to it.[64]

54. [*The Creed: Minimum Content of Faith*]. According to St Thomas, all the baptised are obliged to believe explicitly the articles of the Creed.[65] Therefore, it is not enough to believe in a general saving will of God, but in the incarnation, passion and resurrection of Christ, which is only possible through faith in the Trinitarian God. This is the faith "in which all attain new life," in which every Christian is baptised.[66] At the time of the Fathers, the rule of faith played a similar role: it functioned for all believers as the compendium of the fundamental content, as well as the guideline of verification of the binding elements of faith.[67] St Thomas argues that this knowledge of the faith does not presuppose other prior knowledge, but is accessible to simple people; moreover, because of the festivities of the liturgical year its content is present to everyone. The obligation of an explicit faith in the symbol for all members of the Church means, correlatively, the recognition of the equal dignity of all Christians.

---

[64] Thomas Aquinas, *De ver.* 14, a.11, ad 7.

[65] Thomas Aquinas, *De ver.* 14, a.11, corp.: "tempore vero gratiae omnes, maiores et minores, de Trininate et de redemptore teneretur explicitam fidem habere. Non tamen omnia credibilia circa Trinitatem vel redemptorem minores explicite credere tenentur, sed soli maiores. Minores autem tenentur explicite credere generales articulos, ut Deum esse trinum et unum, filium Dei esse incarnatum, mortuum, et resurrexisse, et alia huiusmodi, de quibus Ecclesia festa facit."

[66] Thomas Aquinas, *ST* II-II, q.2, a.7; a.8.

[67] Cf. e.g. Irenaeus, *Adv. haer.* I, 10, 1 (SCh 264, 154-158); III, 12, 13; III, *pr.* ss.; III, 5,3 (SCh 211, 236-238; 20-22; 60-62); Clement of Alexandria, *Strom.* IV, 1,3 (GCS 15, 249); Tertullian, *Praesc.* 13; 36 (CCSL 1, 197-198; 217); *Prax.* 2; 30 (CCSL 2, 1160; 1204); *Virg.* 1 (CCSL 2, 1209); Origen, *De princ.*, I, *praef.*, 4 (GCS 22, 9-11; FuP 27, 120-124); Novatian, *Trin.* 1, 1; 9, 46 (CCSL 4, 11;25).

55. [*Notes on Lack of Faith*]. The opposite of faith is not the scarcity of knowledge, but the obstinate rejection of some truths of faith[68] and indifference. In this line, Hugh of St Victor clearly distinguishes two groups. There are believers who have little intellectual insight into the faith and who are also not characterised by a deep personal relationship with God, who nevertheless cling to belonging to the ecclesial community and put their faith into practise in their lives.[69]Others, however, are only believers "in name and by custom." These "receive the sacraments together with the other believers, but without any thought for the goods of the world to come."[70] Here a crucial element of the Christian faith is mentioned: whether "future goods are expected" (cf. *Heb* 11:1), and whether this believing hope is strong enough to guide human action.

c) Reciprocity between Faith-Sacraments

56. [*Concept of Sacrament*]. The Triune God, who creates in order to transmit his gifts and who created human persons in order to call them individually and communally to communion with him, enters into relationship with them in a mediated way, through creation and history, through signs, as we have seen. Within these signs, the Christian sacraments occupy a very prominent place, for they are those signs to which God has linked the transmission of his grace in a sure and objective way. In fact, the sacraments of the New Law are effective signs which transmit grace.[71] As we have already said, this does not mean that the sacraments are the only means by which God transmits his grace;[72] it does mean that they hold a privileged position, marked by certainty and ecclesiality. Devotion and personal piety can unfold through different practises: such as different forms of prayer linked to

---

[68] Thomas Aquinas, *ST* II-II, q.5, a.3.

[69] *Sacr.* I pars 10 chap. 3.

[70] *Sacr.* I pars 10 chap. 4.

[71] Cf. *Catechism of the Catholic Church*, 1084.

[72] Thomas Aquinas, *ST* III, q.64, a.7.

Sacred Scripture, such as *lectio* or contemplation of the mysteries of Christ's life; contemplation of God's works in creation and history; and the various sacramentals (cf. §40), etc.

57. [*Faith and Sacraments in Vatican II's Definition of Sacrament*]. Throughout history there have been different definitions of what a sacrament is. Vatican II characterises it this way:

> The purpose of the sacraments is to sanctify men, to build up the body of Christ, and, finally, to give worship to God; because they are signs and they also instruct. They not only presuppose faith, but by words and objects they also nourish, strengthen, and express it; that is why they are called "sacraments of faith." They do indeed impart grace, but, in addition, the very act of celebrating them most effectively disposes the faithful to receive this grace in a fruitful manner, to worship God duly, and to practise charity.[73]

This dense text emphasises several fundamental aspects of the essential reciprocity between faith and sacraments, which we summarise. First, the sacraments have a *pedagogical* purpose for our faith: they illustrate the way salvific history happens: "sacramental." Jesus Christ instituted them to teach us that he communicates himself and transmits his salvation to us in a sensitive and visible way, that is, adapted to the human condition[74] (cf. esp. §§ 20, 26).

Second, the sacraments *presuppose* faith in a twofold sense: as "access" to the sacramental mystery: if faith is lacking, the sacrament appears only as an external symbol or an empty rite, with the risk of slipping into a magical gesture; and as a necessary condition for the sacrament to produce subjectively the gifts it objectively contains. Third, the sacraments *manifest* the faith of the subject and of the Church. The celebration of the sacraments is a profession of lived faith. The sacraments are signs

---

[73] Vatican II, Dogmatic Constitution *Sacrosanctum concilium*, 59.

[74] Cf. St Thomas, *ST* III, q.61, a.1.

by which the faith from which man is justified is professed. The sacramental word requires the response of the faith of the believer who, because of it, learns and recognises the mystery realised in the sacrament. Fourth, the sacraments *nourish* faith on two fundamental levels: they communicate the gift of divine grace, which makes or strengthens the Christian life of the believer; and they are celebrations in which the mystery of salvation is effectively signified, educating the faith and nourishing it continuously. The sacraments are, therefore, signs of faith in all aspects of the dynamism of their realisation: before, during, and after the celebration. Consequently, since the sacraments presuppose faith, it is obvious that the recipient of the sacraments is a member of the Church. We cannot forget that through faith and the sacraments of faith we enter into dialogue, in vital contact with the Redeemer, who is seated at the right hand of the Father. The glorious Christ does not reach us only internally, but in the concretion of our historical being, elevating the fundamental situations of our existence to sacramental situations of salvation.

58. [*Connection Faith and Sacraments*]. Faith is not guaranteed forever at the time of conversion. It is to be cultivated through the practise of charity, prayer, listening to the Word, communal life, instruction, also, and in a pre-eminent place, through the assiduous reception of the sacraments. In the realm of relationships, what is not explicit and expressed runs the risk of being diluted or even disappearing. Christ, the gift, which is the gift of God *par excellence*, cannot be accepted *only* invisibly or privately. On the contrary, he who receives it is empowered and called to incarnate it in his life, word, thought and action. In this way, one contributes to the transformation of the original sacramentality of the Saviour into the fundamental sacramentality of the Church. In truth, the seven fundamental realisations of the Church (the sacraments) realise what they mean. For their reception to be fruitful, however, the willingness of each recipient to deepen, to live and to bear witness to what he or she had received is required.

59. The intrinsic connection between faith and sacraments is evident if we consider other essential aspects. Among them stand out:

a) The sacramental celebration: in which a particular action or material reality, which already has a meaning of its own, is related to the history of salvation and is determined by the event of Christ. Through the Word, the sign becomes the presence, memory and promise of the fulness of salvation.[75] Thus, for example, water as such possesses the property of cleaning. However, only together with the invocation of the Trinity does it produce the regenerating effect of eliminating sins.

b) The terminology: "sacramentum (sacrament)" is used as a translation from the Greek "mystérion (μυστήριον)." The mysteries celebrated in the Church are rooted in the *mystery* as such, "hidden from the beginning of time in God" (*Eph* 3:9) and now are made known: *Christ*. He who, through his incarnation, passion and resurrection, wants to "draw all to himself"(cf. *Jn* 12:32), "to reconcile them to God" (cf. *2 Cor* 5:19-21). According to the letter to the Ephesians (3:3-21 and 5:21-33; cf. *Col* 1:25-27; 2:2-9), the Church is included in the mystery of Christ; as "body" and "bride" she belongs to the "hidden mystery," to the saving plan of God.[76] The New Testament concept of "mystérion" designates the reality of God, who communicates himself to men in Jesus Christ. To the extent that it is an inexhaustible reality, it remains hidden even in the very event of revelation, because it overflows all understanding and conceptualisation. Although the Latin translation "sacramentum" underlines revelation more than concealment, the Latin concept also preserves the dimension of reference to what is inapprehensible. From this it follows that whoever celebrates the liturgy of the Church or receives a sacrament is

---

[75] "Accedit verbum ad elementum et fit sacramentum, etiam ipsum tamquam visibile verbum" (Augustine, *In Johannis ev.*, LXXX, 3; CCSL 36, 529; PL 35, 1840).

[76] Cf. Augustine, *Epist.* 187, 34 (PL 33, 846).

called to transcend, through his personally believed faith, the content believed towards the ever greater mystery.

c) There is a second aspect also relating to the very revealing terminology. Originally *sacramentum* means a "sacred oath" which, in contrast with "ius iurandum," produces a sacred bond. This is the meaning that Tertullian has in mind when he calls baptism "sacrament"[77] and compares it to the commitment made by the military in the flag pledge. It is not possible to resolve to something without knowing what its content is.

60. [*Need for Catechesis*]. From what has already been said, we start from a double base. First, there can be no sacramental celebration without faith. Second, personal faith is a participation in ecclesial faith, a response to the sacramental event of revelation witnessed to and proposed by the Church, thanks to the Spirit. Therefore, since the reception of a sacrament is simultaneously an act of a strictly personal nature and of a manifestly ecclesial nature, an adequate catechesis must precede the celebration of the sacrament. In such catechesis, the paschal mystery must occupy a preponderant place because of its centrality in the Christian faith. In the case of baptism, catechesis is part of the very incorporation into the Church, as perceived in the development of the catechumenate in the ancient Church. From another perspective, the primitive form of baptism included a confession of faith, in the form of dialogue, as *Traditio apostolica* testifies.[78] The confession of faith and the divine-human dialogical nature of the reception of the sacraments must continue through the mystagogical catechesis, which takes place at each reception of the sacraments. In a certain way, mystagogical catechesis supposes entering into the eschatological presence that happens with the sacraments, progressing in a continuous way in knowledge through participation in the celebrated mysteries.

---

[77] Tertullian, *Ad mart.* 3 (CCSL 1,5).

[78] *Traditio apostolica*, 16 (entry into the catechumenate), 17-20 (course of the catechumenate), 21 (baptismal celebration; SCh 11, 43-51).

61. [*Manifestation of Faith*]. The sacraments are part of the sacramental economy into which the believer is introduced. This economy implies the existence of visible aspects as an expression of invisible grace. Although faith in God revealed in Christ is a gift of grace, the recipient is not a mere object of this gift. This is why Thomas Aquinas makes it clear that faith is a "virtus infusa vel supranaturalis." As "virtue," faith is a capacity to act made possible by grace which, like every faculty, can be perfected. In other words, the deeper the relationship of a believer with Christ, the more intense is the sacramentality of this faith, his prayer, his confession, his identification with the Church and his love. Consequently, since faith is a virtue, it must be manifested externally, in a visible way, in a style of life corresponding to the double commandment of love of God and neighbour, and in a relationship with the praying Church.

62. There can be a generic faith, as assent to divine revelation, without including in itself the hope in God and the love of God which is inherent in it. The scholastic distinction between "fides informis" and "fides (caritate) formata" reflects the problem of a faith that has not yet reached the degree of maturity that is essential to it. According to the letter to the Hebrews, faith is necessary for salvation: "without faith it is impossible to please [God]" (*Heb* 11:6); this is a conviction rooted in the understanding of faith in the Middle Ages.[79] While a mere desire to believe what is true (*fides informis*) does not ground a communion with Christ, the loving faith (*fides caritate formata*) produces rooting in the participation of the salvific and blessed reality of God. In other words, a form of faith can be given that is not internally shaped by a personal relationship with Christ. In that sense it is considered *informis*: it is not informed in its configuration by the love of Christ, as a response to his first love. There is also a kind of faith that is moulded by a personal and loving relationship with Christ. That is why it is called *caritate formata*: configured

---

[79] "Fidei obiectum per se est id per quod homo beatus efficitur" (*ST* II-II, q. 2, a.5; cf. *ST* II-II, q.1, a.6 ad 1).

51

by the charity that is inherent in the truth of the relationship that faith wants to express.

63. Following this distinction, it can be established that loving faith is indeed the beginning of eternal life.[80] The personal act of believing (*actus credendi*) and the virtue of faith (*virtus fidei*) are the ones that produce, on their own, that the salvific event is effective in the believer. Now, the act of faith is not possible without the affirmation of that reality that makes it possible. This being so, however, the reception of every sacrament does not presuppose a faith formed by charity, as is particularly emphasised in the sacrament of penance. In the opinion of Thomas Aquinas, neither baptism nor marriage requires the same measure of faith impregnated with love as the Eucharist. The fruitful reception of Holy Communion presupposes not only faith in the real presence of Christ in the sacramental species, but also the will to maintain the bond of union with Christ and with his members (cf. §120).

64. Because supernatural love (*caritas*) is an immediate effect of grace, the presence of a "fides caritate formata" on the basis of human criteria cannot be ascertained. Consequently, no one can know with certainty about another person, not even about himself, if his faith possesses this quality. This can only be inferred from clues or effects.[81] Therefore, there can be no question of making a judgement about how a person presents himself before God or of wanting to confirm or deny belief as a supernatural gift of grace in another person. However, since the reception of a sacrament is an ecclesial public act, the external and visible is decisive: that is, the intention expressed, confession of faith, and the fidelity to the baptismal promise in life.

---

[80] "inchoatio vitae aeternae in nobis" (*ST* II-II, q.4, a.1).

[81] Cf. Bonaventure, III *Sent. Dist* 23 dub.4 (III 504ab) ; II *Sent. dist.* 38 dub.1 (II 894b); Thomas Aquinas, *ST* I-II, q.112, a.5; *De Ver* 10 a.10 ad 1.2.8.

d) Dialogical Nature of the Sacraments

65. [*Faith, Validity and Fecundity*]. The Council of Trent (DH 1608) has used the term "ex opere operato" to express the following. When a sacrament is celebrated in an appropriate manner, in the name of the Church and in accordance with the meaning given to it by the Church, in that case it always conveys what it signifies. This clarification does not imply foregoing the participation of the one who dispenses and receives the sacrament. On the contrary: he who dispenses a sacrament must have the intention of doing what the Church does (DH 1611: *faciendi quod facit ecclesia*). On the part of the receiver, a distinction must be made between fruitful (fertile) and unfruitful (infecunda). The term "opus operatum" is not directed against the participation of the person administering the sacrament or of the person receiving it. It emphasises that neither the faith of the one who dispenses nor of the one who receives the sacrament produces salvation, but only the sacramentally mediated grace of the Redeemer. It is not the case, then, that because those who dispense the sacrament and those who receive it believe in what they do in the sacrament, then, for that very reason, Christ acts through the sacrament. But it is the case of the following: whenever a sacrament is celebrated in an appropriate way, according to the meaning given to it by the Church, Christ links its action to that of the Church.

66. In this sense, faced with the theology of the reformers, the Council of Trent will clearly affirm the efficacy of the sacraments.[82] However, an ecclesial practise that only attends to the validity damages the sacramental organism of the Church, because it reduces it to one of its essential aspects. A valid sacrament transmits what technical terminology has called "res et sacramentum," as a constitutive part of the sacramental action of grace. For example, in the case of baptism it would be the

---

[82] "Si quis dixerit, sacramenta...aut gratiam ipsam non ponentibus obicem non conferre...anathema sit" (Council of Trent, Session 7, "Decrees on the sacraments," canon 6 [DH 1606]).

"character." However, the sacraments point to and obtain their full meaning in the transmission of the "res," of the grace proper to the sacrament. In the case of baptism, it points to the grace of new life in Christ, which includes the forgiveness of sins.

67. [*Adequate Faith for the Sacraments and Intention*]. Sacramental logic includes, as an essential constituent, the free response, the acceptance of God's gift, in one word: faith, however incipient it may be, especially in the case of baptism. The most recent theology has taken as a reference to illuminate the transmission of grace that takes place in the sacraments the world of signification, proper to symbols and signs. This field is situated in an order very close to human language and interpersonal relations. Since the sacraments are located in the dialogical and relational realm of the believer with Christ, this approach has its advantages. The signification of symbols or signs is not grasped if one does not participate in the world that the symbol in its signification creates. Similarly, it is not possible to receive the effects of sacramental grace (fruitfulness or fecundity), conveyed by sacramental signs, without entering into the world that these sacramental signs express. Faith is the key that opens the entrance into that world that makes sacramental realities truly become signs that signify and efficaciously cause divine grace.

68. The reception of the sacraments can be valid or invalid, fruitful or fruitless. For an adequate disposition it is not enough not to contradict either externally or internally what the sacrament means. In this sense, a valid reception does not automatically imply a fruitful reception of the sacrament. For a fruitful reception, a positive intention is required. In other words, the recipient must believe both in the content (*fides quae*) and existentially (*fides qua*) that which Christ gives him sacramentally through the mediation of the Church. There is a diversity of degrees of conformity with the doctrine. What is decisive here is that the recipient does not reject the Church's

teaching at all. There are also degrees as to the intensity of faith. What is decisive here is the positive disposition to receive what the sacrament signifies. Each fruitful reception of a sacrament is a communicative act and therefore part of the dialogue between Christ and the individual believer.

69. While it is true that the doctrine about intention arose out of reflections on the indispensable requirements of ministers who dispense the sacraments, the intention stands at a crucial point. On the one hand, it completely saves the efficacy "ex opere operato," that is: the efficacy of sacramental actions is due wholly and exclusively to Christ and not to the faith of either the recipient or the minister of the sacrament. But it also leaves open the dialogical nature of the sacramental event, so that one does not fall into either magic or sacramental automatism. The intention expresses the indispensable minimum of voluntary personal participation in the gratuitous event of the sacramental transmission of saving grace.

70. Sacramental symbols and symbolic actions, performed through water, oil, bread, wine, and other visible and external factors, invite each believer to open the "inner eye of faith"[83] and see the saving effects of each sacrament. These symbolic actions, carried out with these material elements, are, in reality, in function of performing an action of Christ, the Saviour. What happens in the administration of the sacraments is rooted in what happened in the actions of Christ, the Saviour, in his earthly life, such as in healings. Many believed in Christ (*Ur-Sacrament*) and thus attained sanctification, such as: the Samaritan woman at Jacob's well (*Jn* 4:28-29; 30); Zacchaeus, when he received Jesus into his house (*Lk* 19:8-10); the Syrophoenecian woman, who obtained healing for her daughter by an unshakable faith (*Mk* 7:24-30), and so on. These symbolic, "sacramental" actions of Jesus, carried out with material elements, were in function of the intensification of faith in the beneficiaries and sanctification,

---

[83] Ephrem, *Hymni de fide*, 53, 12; 5, 18 (CSCO 154, 167, 23 ; 155, 143, 17).

thanks to the internal faith-vision. The strengthened faith must be translated into a believing confession through the Christian witness of life in the world.

71. [*Dialogical Nature*]. The liturgical celebration of the sacraments not only describes God's katabatic (descending) salvific action, but also, inseparable from the former, the anabatic (ascending) movement of the recipient, beginning with the "amen" response to gestures, such as the extension of the hands in the reception of communion. All the sacraments are *communicative* actions, inscribed within the economy of salvation: of the historical unfolding of God's desire to enter into a personal relationship with men. Thus, in the sacraments, the *covenant* nature that marks and accompanies the whole history of salvation is reflected. Where the dialogical nature of the sacrament diminishes, misunderstandings of a magical type (ritualism) and centred on individual salvation (subjectivist privatisation) arise.

e) The Sacramental Organism

72. [*The Sacramental Organism*]. The sacramental organism of the Church,[84] shaped through an evolution of centuries, attends to the key circumstances of the life of the individual person and of the community in order to strengthen the Christian in his faith, to insert him more vividly into the mystery of Christ and of the Church, accompanying him and strengthening him throughout the whole journey of his life of faith. Not only does it gather dense moments of the unfolding of the mystery of Christ in his earthly life, but by making them sacramentally present, it makes his work continue. In this way, the original sacramentality of Christ, through the sacramental celebrations of the Church, reaches out to the individual believer and makes him the living sacrament of Christ. Thanks to water, bread, wine, oil and sacramental words, which contain a meaning of direct reference to Christ and make it a reality, the believer is fully inserted into

---

[84] Cf. *Catechism of the Catholic Church*, 1076.

this reality and is configured by it provided that he accepts these signs with the proper dispositions.

73. [*Sacraments of Initiation*]. The sacraments of initiation, situated at the beginning of the journey, insert the believer fully in Christ and in the ecclesial community, enabling him, with grace, to be in some way the sacrament of Christ with his life. Thus, baptism is the gateway. Being buried in the waters and coming out of them expresses participation in Christ's death and resurrection, entering into his Body and being conformed to him, becoming a living and active member of Christ's Church (cf. *infra* chap. 3.1.). Confirmation, with the reception of the chrism, implies a further step in the same direction. The anointing with the chrism, in parallel with the anointing of Christ, empowers the Christian by the gift of the Spirit to witness to the faith by assuming this responsibility in the Christian community with a more missionary and ecclesial faith (cf. *infra* chapter 3.2.). Through the Eucharist, the sacrament of the Body of Christ, insertion, communion and full participation in the Body of Christ is expressed in all senses: Christological, sacramental and ecclesial (cf. *infra* chapter 3.3.). At the end of initiation, the Christian is already a member of Christ and his Church, having received all the ordinary means of christification, which enable him to lead a Christian life and to bear true witness.

74. [*Sacraments of Healing*]. Those who receive the sacraments of initiation do not always behave with full fidelity and integrity with regard to what is signified in them. For this reason, there are also sacraments called sacraments of healing, which bear in mind our fragility and sin. With penance, upon receiving the welcome of the minister, who represents Christ and the Church, and pronounces in the name of Christ and the Church the words of absolution, not only does reconciliation with God take place, after having denied him with his own life, but also with the ecclesial body which proclaims the goodness of God in Jesus Christ as a community of the forgiven. Thus, thanks to penance,

the Christian straightens out again his journey of faith. Since the Eucharist is the sacrament of the Body of Christ par excellence, it makes no sense for those who, having seriously damaged what insertion into this Body means, have not received the gift of forgiveness which reconciles with God and joyfully reintegrated into community membership, to participate fully in it.

75. The Anointing of the Sick is celebrated in a situation of fragility, such as illness. Christ's chrism, healing ointment and fragrance, expresses the Lord's strength to save the whole person and bring him to his glory, even though there would have been serious failures (sins) of incoherence with the life of faith, expressly including forgiveness (cf. *Jas* 5:14-15). Thus, it is testified that even sickness can be an occasion for the manifestation of the glory of God (*Jn* 11:4); and that, in sickness, in life and in death we are of the Lord (*Rom* 14:8-9) by sharing with him his passion and sufferings on the way to glory. In this way, both sin and sickness become an occasion to grow in union with the Lord and to witness that his mercy is stronger than our fragility.

76. [*Sacraments at the Service of Communion*]. Other sacraments look more directly at the service of communion. The community requires a structure and a government that reflects its sacramental reality. For this reason, ministers ordained *ad sacerdotium* represent Christ the Head. They configure themselves expressly with him through the exercise of pastoral charity. Thus Christ continues to be present in his Church not only as the gift which begot her, but also sacramentally as the one who continually gives himself to her, incessantly begetting her anew. Furthermore, from another perspective and as members of the Church, ordained ministers also represent the Church, especially in their liturgical prayer, praising God and beseeching his grace on behalf of all. Thus, Christ the Shepherd and Head continues to edify his Body in history. The whole Church recognises in the ordained ministry, over and over again, how it

is due to the gift of the Lord, in his Word and in his sacraments, while the ordained ministers are to conform their life to Christ to be pastors according to his heart.

77. Those who have been born again of water and the Spirit exercise their common priesthood (cf. LG 10), inseparable from the life of faith, also in the love they profess to each other as spouses. The love publicly professed by the spouses is a sacred bond with which they make Christ's love for us his Church historically visible and present in the world. In this way, thanks to marriage, the Christian community grows and children are begotten, fruit of love, who, by breathing faith in the family, increase the number of members of the Body of Christ. Thus the family becomes the domestic Church, the preponderant place for the reception, living and expression of faith (cf. *infra* chapter 4).

f) The Reciprocity between Faith and the Sacraments in the Sacramental Economy

78. This joint review of the reciprocity between faith and the sacraments in the sacramental economy has shown us several aspects of great importance for our topic.

a) In the divine economy everything starts from the salvific revelation of the Trinitarian God. This economy reaches its peak when the Father reveals his Son through the Pasch of the Son and the gift of the Spirit at Pentecost. These salvific mysteries are perpetuated in history through the Church and the sacraments thanks to the action of the Spirit.

b) This revelation and communication of God has a sacramental nature: invisible grace is transmitted through visible signs. The sacramental nature of revelation is perceived through faith.

c) Faith is a personal relationship with the Trinitarian God, through which one responds to his grace, to his sacramental revelation. Therefore, faith is essential and constitutively dialogical. It is also a dynamic reality that accompanies the whole life of the believer. As in any relationship it is possible to grow and strengthen itself, but also its opposites: to weaken or even get lost. At the same time, it has a personal and ecclesial imprint. Since the personal relationship with the Trinitarian God is already lived with faith, faith leads to salvation and eternal life.

d) God's salvific action, the economy, extends beyond the visible frontiers of the Church. This factor would seem to deny the sacramental nature of the economy. However, a careful consideration of the way salvation works in such cases shows that God's salvific action, welcomed by an implicit type of faith, is not done outside the sacramentality of the divine economy, but precisely because of it.[85]

e) Under different figures and aspects, the celebration of the sacraments must always be accompanied by faith in its various aspects: a personal faith, which, in its dynamism towards God, participates in the ecclesial faith and adheres to it through the desired ecclesial belonging or, at the very least, makes its own the specific ecclesial intention inherent in sacramental celebrations. In this way, the sacramental celebration never falls into a sacramental automatism.

f) Faith itself has, in its very essence, a natural tendency to express itself and nourish itself sacramentally, precisely because of the sacramental structure of the economy which gives rise to it. Not only should faith in the saving grace of Jesus Christ (*Ur-Sacrament*) not be opposed to its historical permanence in space and time thanks to the Church (*Grundsakrament*), but it should not even be denoted as separate.

---

[85] Congregation for the Doctrine of the Faith, Declaration *Dominus Iesus* (6th August 2000) 20-22: AAS 92 (2000), 761-764. See our § 37.

2.3. CONCLUSION: DYNAMISMS OF FAITH AND SACRAMENTALITY

79. In short, we can conclude with a series of outstanding dynamisms, which have risen from the consideration of the dialogical nature of the sacramental economy:

a) Faith constitutes the dialogical response to the sacramental interlocution of the Trinitarian God. This factor seals the reciprocity between faith and sacraments. In the journey of the believer, faith is modulated and expressed in the various situations of life, accompanied by the various sacraments that the Church offers for the Christian life throughout the earthly pilgrimage.

b) By its own constitution, the Christian faith is sacramental. For this reason, there is a connaturality between faith and sacramentality. One of the fundamental dynamisms of faith consists, then, in its sacramental expression, as a way of nourishing, strengthening, enriching and manifesting itself.

c) In the sacramental expression of faith, both the personal (subjective) and the ecclesial (objective) dimensions of faith come into play. In its dynamism of growth, personal faith adheres more intensely and is more identified with ecclesial faith. Reciprocity between faith and sacraments excludes the possibility of a sacramental celebration totally alien to ecclesial faith (intention).

d) The sacramentality proper to faith always entails a missionary dynamism, because it actively inscribes the believer in the dynamics of the divine economy, endowing him with a certain leading role, for which divine grace empowers. Those who receive a sacrament intensify their christification thanks to the Spirit, reaffirm their ecclesial insertion and perform a liturgical act of praise to God, who distributes his goods to us through the sacraments. From this point of view, it is understood, for example, that those who receive baptism are, in the first place, gratuitously graced: they are configured to the paschal mystery of Christ; but at the same time, they are called to bear witness to the gift received through a life of praise that springs from the faith of the Church. No one receives the sacraments exclusively for himself, but also to represent and strengthen the Church, which, as a means and instrument of Christ (cf. LG 1), must be a credible witness and an effective sign of hope against all hope, witnessing for the world the salvation of Christ, God's sacrament par excellence. Thus, through the celebration of the sacraments and their adequate living, the Body of Christ is strengthened.

3. RECIPROCITY BETWEEN FAITH AND SACRAMENTS IN CHRISTIAN INITIATION

80. [*Introduction*]. Once we have seen the reigning essential reciprocity between faith and sacraments on a general double plane, from the sacramental economy and from faith and the sacraments, we move on to consider their incidence on the sacraments of Christian initiation. It is therefore a question of applying the notions and points of view gained in order to make them bear fruit in each of the three sacraments of initiation. Each sacrament has its own specificity, which is to be respected. However, in order to systematise the treatment of the main question, we proceed according to five articulated steps, with exceptions adapted to each sacrament. These steps are: (1) the principal biblical foundation; (2) the correlation between the said sacrament and the appropriate faith for the celebration thereof; (3) the problems that arise today around this correlation; (4) the illumination starting from the distinguished and chosen moments of the Tradition; and, in the light of the preceding reflection on the place of faith in the celebration of the sacrament, (5) a theological proposal ordered to pastoral care about the faith necessary for the celebration of each sacrament. Due to the differential problem of baptism of adults and children, this scheme is adapted to each case. We start from the baptism of adults and complete the treatment with the specific elements of the baptism of children. We presuppose a more complete theology of each sacrament. We simply collect some essential elements to articulate a meaningful response to the question of reciprocity between faith and sacrament in each of the sacraments of initiation.

3.1. RECIPROCITY BETWEEN FAITH AND BAPTISM

a) Biblical Foundation

81. After the great kerygmatic preaching on the day of Pentecost, the listeners were "pierced in their heart, and they asked Peter and the other apostles: 'What are we do to, brethren?' Peter answered them: 'Repent and let every one of you be baptised in the name of Jesus, the Messiah, for the forgiveness of your sins; and you will receive the gift of the Holy Spirit.' [...] Those who accepted his words were baptised" (*Acts* 2:37-38, 41). Conversion, the human response to the proclamation of the Gospel, seems inseparable from the sacramental rite of baptism, which is linked to several fundamental aspects of Christian life. Through baptism, the believer participates in the paschal mystery of Christ (cf. *Rom* 6:1-11), anticipated by Christ in his own baptism and realised in his passion and resurrection (cf. *Mk* 10:38; *Lk* 12:50); the believer is clothed in Christ, is configured to him, becomes in Christ and with Christ. Thus, we become adopted sons and new creatures. The apostle Paul also understand that with baptism:

> Christians have been entrusted to a "standard of teaching" (*týpos didachés*), which they now obey from the heart (cf. *Rom* 6:17). In baptism we receive both a teaching to be professed and a specific way of life which demands the engagement of the whole person and sets us on the path to goodness. Those who are baptised are set in a new context, entrusted to a new environment, a new and shared way of acting, in the Church.[86]

One is also incorporated into the Church, the body of Christ (cf. *1 Cor* 1: 11-16; 12:13). Through baptism, one receives the promised Holy Spirit (*Acts* 1:5), forgiveness of sins (*Col* 2:12-13), justification. In this way, the newly baptised, the new creature, by this new birth (*Jn* 3:3, 5) belongs to Christ and to the Church, is able to live the Christian life, witnessing to it with a new life.

---

[86] Francis, Encyclical Letter *Lumen fidei* (29th June 2013) 41 : AAS 105 (2013), 583.

b) Faith and Adult Baptism

82. Baptism is the sacrament of faith par excellence. Already Mark 16:16 links faith and baptism: "He who believes and is baptised will be saved." In addition, the baptismal mandate with which Matthew's Gospel ends (28:19) contains a baptismal formula, in which the Church has seen the synthesis of her Trinitarian faith. On the other hand, the rite of baptism clearly reflects the importance of faith. In the current rite of acceptance into the catechumenate, the catechumen asks the Church for "the faith" that gives "eternal life."[87] In the ancient Church, the rite of triple immersion was accompanied by responses to an interrogative creed.[88] Today, the renunciations and profession of faith are an integral part of the rite. The ritual celebration itself, with its scrutinies, highlights the dialogical nature of the event: the public proclamation of the faith of the catechumen, previously tested during the catechumenate in its various phases, and the reception of the baptism given by an ecclesial minister. The scrutinies themselves fulfil the function of ensuring the adherence to the ecclesial faith on the part of the one being baptised, beyond the previous demonstrations of knowledge of the doctrine, conformity with the morals and practise of prayer during the catechumenate. Being a gift of God, no one administers a sacrament to himself. Just as faith is received through preaching and listening to the Word, so too the sacraments are part of this logic of receiving God's gift.

83. The Christian thus configured to Christ continues his pilgrimage in faith, receiving on other occasions the Holy Spirit in the celebration of the other sacraments and other sacramentals. Two analogies illuminate this reality. The infusion of the "breath of life" by God upon Adam (*Gn* 2:7). Most importantly, the whole public ministry of Jesus is marked by the reception of the Spirit sent by the Father. It is the Spirit with whom he was anointed in baptism (*Mk* 1:10 and similar), and who led him into the desert

---

[87] *Rite of Christian Initiation of Adults*, §75; cf. Ibid., §247.

[88] *Traditio apostolica*, 21 (SCh 11, 50-51).

(*Mk* 1:12 and similar), with whom he proclaimed to be anointed in the synagogue of Nazareth (*Lk* 4:16-21); and through whom he expelled demons (*Mt* 12.28), and whom he exhaled on the cross (*Mt* 27:50; *Lk* 23:46).As a whole, his entire mission can be described as a baptism, with reference to Easter (cf. *Lk* 12:50). In this way, the life of the Christian is understood as a progressive unfolding of that which the initial gift of the Spirit in baptism sets in motion, up to the consummation of one's own life, giving it to the Father, like Jesus.

c) Pastoral Proposal: Faith for Adult Baptism

84. With baptism, the sacrament of new life in Christ[89] and new birth, one embarks on a journey, becomes part of the Church and enters into the sacramental economy. In the ancient Church, this change of life was expressed visibly and bodily, with the baptised turning from the West, where one looked during the renunciations, towards the East, during the profession of faith. There has always been a request for preparation through the catechumenate or other forms of instruction, but there has also been a good awareness of the initial nature of the baptismal faith. For this reason, the previous catechumenal process must have been followed with seriousness and assiduity, with the catechumen proclaiming in a responsible way his adhesion to the Trinitarian faith received and the desire to continue progressing in the knowledge of it and in the coherence of life with it, thanks to the gift of baptismal grace. Baptism being the door of entry, the faith required for baptism does not have to be perfect, but initial and eager to grow.

85. Just as the catechumenate is understood as a part of initiation, so baptism does not consist of a rite closed in on itself, but requires from its own internal dynamic a display of life as baptised. Nor has the understanding of the faith been closed, despite the equality between the faith that is celebrated in the rite and the faith that is believed.[90] This corresponds to post-baptismal catechesis, in a sense as a further phase of instruction specifically dedicated

---

[89] Augustine, *Sermo VIII in octava Paschatis ad infantes*, 1 (PL 46, 838).

[90] Cf. Basil the Great, *De Spiritu Sancto* XI, 27 (SCh 17bis, 340-342).

to the sacrament. The practise of the ancient Church reflects the conviction that the true understanding of the *"mysteria"* occurs after their reception.[91] In any case, it was not assumed that the understanding happened by itself, but that neophytes were introduced to the sacraments through mystagogical catechesis.

86. [*Lights from the Tradition*]. Cyril of Jerusalem insistently tells of the conversion of the heart and warns: "If your intention remains wrong (...) then you will receive the water, but not the Holy Spirit."[92] It does not explicitly demand the strength of faith in the sense of an extraordinary force capable of moving mountains, but believing adherence to the ecclesial proclamation: "You need faith, which depends on you, faith in God, so that you may receive the faith that God grants and works superhuman things."[93] Faith can and must grow; the willingness to do so belongs to the very decision to be baptised.[94]

87. When, starting from the Constantinian turning-point, the classical catechumenate, with its seriousness and its various stages, was gradually disappearing, the Church adapted to a new circumstance: society became mainly Christian. In this situation, general socialisation included a certain religious socialisation, at least comparatively greater than at the previous epoch. However, the need continued for an ecclesial figure of the faith (godparents); and of a previous minimum instruction, that allowed a responsible and conscious personal adhesion. The case of the Indies is instructive. In spite of the fact that different tendencies existed and that in the theology of the time salvation was closely linked with baptism, one ended up with the opinion that best safeguarded the dignity of the Indians and the dialogical nature

---

[91] Cyril of Jerusalem, *Catecheses mystagogicae*, I, 1 (PG 33, 1065; SCh 126, 84).

[92] *Procatech*. Introd. n. 4 (PG 33, 340A).

[93] *Procatech*. V, 11 (PG 33, 520B).

[94] *Procatech*. I, 6; I, 4 (bear fruit; PG 33, 377 and 373-376). Above all in the catechesis of John Chrysostom to the neophytes: *Cat.* 3/5, 2. 15. 21 (FC 6/2, 412-415, 424ff., 428-431); *Cat.* 3/7, 16-25 (FC 6/2, 478-487) among others, there are warnings against negligence and lukewarmness.

of the sacraments.[95] Along these lines, the Dominican, Francisco de Vitoria, together with other theologians, wrote a report on the question of the adequate preparation of the Christians of the new continent, in the midst of an enormous shortage of priests, on whom fell the burden of catechesis:

> They are not be baptised before they have been sufficiently instructed not only in the faith, but also in Christian mores, at least insofar as it is necessary for salvation. They are not to be baptised before it is likely that they understand what they receive or before they respond and confess in baptism and they wish to live and persevere in the faith and Christian religion.[96]

88. [*Pastoral Proposal*]. The Church is always eager to celebrate baptism. It implies the joy that new believers receive justification, are incorporated into Christ, recognise him as their Saviour, shape their life with Christ, become part of the Church, witness to the new life in the Spirit, with which they have been graced and enlightened. However, in the absolute absence of personal faith, the sacramental rite loses its meaning. While validity is based on the realisation of the sacrament by the minister with the appropriate intention (cf. §§ 65-70), without a minimum of faith on the part of the baptised the essential reciprocity between faith and sacraments fades away. Without faith that visible signs (*sacramentum tantum*) transmit invisible grace (e.g. immersion in water as a transition from death to life), these signs do not transmit the invisible reality signified (*res sacramenti*): forgiveness of sins, justification, rebirth in Christ through the Spirit, entry into filial life. In this case, baptism becomes a mere social convention or is impregnated with pagan elements.

---

[95] Cf. Paul III, Constitution *Altitudo divini consilii* (1st June 1537).

[96] "Parecer de los teólogos de la Universidad de Salamanca sobre el bautismo de los Indios," en *Colección de documentos inéditos, relativos al descubrimiento, conquista y colonización de las posesiones españolas en América y Oceanía*, t. III, Madrid 1865, 545; see full report: 543-553.

89. This minimum of faith seems indispensable for those who receive the sacrament to approach the intention of realising what the Church believes. Some of the elements belonging to this minimum of faith can be deduced from the very dynamic of the sacramental celebration[97]: the Trinitarian faith, with the invocation of the Three Divine Persons on the neophyte; the conviction of being reborn in Christ, symbolised by immersion in the waters, as waters of life;[98] the birth to a new life, signified by the covering with the white vestment; the confidence of receiving the light of Christ and the desire to witness to it, represented by the reception of the light of the paschal candle.

90. Fidelity to the doctrine of the Church, charity and pastoral prudence, together with creativity in welcoming and offering catechumenal itineraries, are therefore required. Not defending sufficiently what the sacrament is and means, for fear of minimum requirements, implies a greater damage to the sacramentality of faith and of the Church. It is detrimental to the integrity and coherence of the very faith that it is intended to safeguard. Certainly the faith of the recipient is not the cause of the grace at work in the sacrament, but it is part of the adequate disposition necessary for the fruitfulness of the sacrament, so that it may be fruitful. Without any kind of faith, it seems difficult to affirm that the indispensable minimum is maintained with respect to the disposition, which includes, at its lowest level, not putting any impediment.[99] In this sense, without a minimum of faith, the gift of God which makes the baptised person the living "sacrament" of Christ, as a letter from Christ (cf. *2 Cor* 3:3), does not succeed in producing the fruit which is proper to him. On the other hand, he who confesses Christ as his Lord and Saviour will not hesitate to associate himself as intimately as possible, sacramentally, with the central nucleus of the saving mystery of Christ: Easter.

---

[97] Cf. Francis, Encyclical Letter *Lumen fidei* (29th June 2013) 42 : AAS 105 (2013), 583-584.

[98] Cf. Is 33:16, read by the *Epistula Barnabae*, 11:5 (SCh 172, 162). Cited by Francis, Encyclical Letter *Lumen fidei* (29th June 2013) 42: AAS 105 (2013), 584.

[99] Council of Trent, Session 7. *Decrees on the Sacraments*, canon 6 (DH 1606). See note 82.

d) Faith and Baptism of Children

91. The baptism of infants has been attested since ancient times.[100] It is justified in the desire of parents that their children participate in sacramental grace, be incorporated into Christ and the Church, become members of the community of God's children as they are of the family, for baptism is an effective means of salvation, forgiving sins, beginning with original sin, and transmitting grace. The child does not knowingly sign his or her membership in his or her natural family, nor is he or she proud of it, as is often the case with many initiation rites, such as circumcision in the Jewish faith. If socialisation follows its ordinary course, it will do so as a young and adult, with gratitude. With the baptism of infants, it is emphasised that the faith in which we are baptised is the ecclesial faith, that our growth in faith takes place thanks to the insertion in the community "we."[101] The celebration confirms it solemnly after the profession of faith: "This is our faith; this is the faith of the Church that we are proud to profess."[102] On this occasion, the parents act as representatives of the Church, which welcomes these children into its bosom.[103] For this reason, the baptism of children is justified from the responsibility of educating in the faith that the parents and godparents contract, parallel to the responsibility of educating them in the rest of the spheres of life.

---

[100] Cf. Irenaeus, *Adv. haer.* II, 22, 4 (SCh 294, 220); Origen, *In Rom.* V, 9 (PG 14, 1047); Cyprian, *Epist.* 64 (CSEL 3, 717-721); Augustine, *De Genesi ad lit.* X, 23, 39 (PL 34, 426); *De peccatorum meritis et remissione et de baptismo parvulorum* I, 26, 39 (PL 44, 131). See also Congregation for the Doctrine of the Faith, Instruction *Pastoralis actio*: AAS 72 (1980) 1137-1156.

[101] Cf. Francis, Encyclical Letter *Lumen fidei* (29th June 2013) 43 : AAS 105 (2013), 584.

[102] *Rite for Baptism of Children*, 127, 152.

[103] "Sicut pueri in maternis uteris constituti non per seipsos nutrimentum accipiunt, sed ex nutrimento matris sustentantur, ita etiam pueri non habentes usum rationis, *quasi in utero matris Ecclesiae constituti*, non per seipsos, sed per actum Ecclesiae salute suscipiunt" (St Thomas Aquinas, *ST* III, q.68, a.9 ad 1). Emphasis added.

e) Pastoral Proposal: Faith for the Baptism of Children

92. Many families live the faith and pass it on to their children, both explicitly and implicitly, whom they educate in the faith having baptised them shortly after being born, following an ancestral Christian custom. However, there are a number of problems. In some places, the number of baptisms decreases drastically. In countries with a Christian tradition, it is not unusual for children preparing for first communion to discover at that time that they are not baptised. Very often some parents request baptism for their children by social convention or family pressure, without participating in the life of the Church and with serious doubts about the intention and ability to provide a future education in the faith of their children.

93. [*Lights from the Tradition*]. With great continuity, the Church has defended the legitimacy of infant baptism, in spite of the criticisms that this practise has received since ancient times. In very early times, we are told of baptisms of entire families (cf. *Acts* 16:15, 33). The tradition of infant baptism is very old. It is already witnessed by the *Apostolic Tradition*.[104] A synod of Carthage, from the year 252, defends it.[105] Tertullian's well-known challenge to the baptism of infants only makes sense if it was a widespread custom.[106] This practise has always been accompanied by a significant ecclesial figure close to the children (parents, godparents), who committed themselves to provide education in the faith along with the ordinary education of the children. Moreover, to the extent that infant baptism became the most regular practise, the need for a post-baptismal catechesis to instruct the baptised in the faith, and thus contribute to avoiding as far as possible their total estrangement or distancing from the faith, was accentuated.[107] Without this representative figure of

---

[104] *Traditio apostolica*, 21 (SCh 11, 49).

[105] Cf. Cyprian, *Epistula* 64, 2-6 (CSEL 3/2, 718-721).

[106] Cf. Tertullian, *De baptismo*, 18, 4-6 (CCSL 1, 293; SCh 35, 92-93).

[107] Cf. Isidore of Seville, *De ecclesiasticis officiis*, II, 21-27; Thomas Aquinas, *ST* II-II, q.10, a.12.

the ecclesial faith, baptism, a sacrament of faith with a marked dialogical nature, would lack one of its essential components.

94. [*Pastoral Proposal*]. In the case of children, there must be a hope based on education in the faith, thanks to the faith of the adults who take responsibility. Without any hope in a future education in the faith, the minimum conditions for a meaningful reception of baptism are not met.[108]

3.2. RECIPROCITY BETWEEN FAITH AND CONFIRMATION

a) Biblical and Historical Foundation

95. [*Biblical Foundation*]. Like baptism, the sacrament of confirmation also finds its foundation in Scripture. This Spirit, as we said, plays a crucial role in the life and mission of Jesus (cf. § 83). It also occupies a stellar place in the Christian life. The disciples are to be clothed with the "power from on high" (*Lk* 24:46-49; *Acts* 1:4-5, 8) before they become witnesses of the Risen One. According to Acts, the Spirit descended on the disciples (*Acts* 2:1-11) and on many others, including the Gentiles (*Acts* 10:45), who thus proclaimed and witnessed to Christ and the Gospel (*Acts* 2:43; 5:12; 6:8; 14:3; 15:12; cf. *Rom* 15:13). The promised Paraclete (*Jn* 14:16; 15:26; 16:7) helps the disciples to progress in their life of faith and bear witness to it before the world. In some passages, a distinction is made between the reception of baptism and a subsequent outpouring of the Spirit, linked to the intervention of the apostles through the laying on of hands on Christians who already live their faith (cf. *Acts* 8:14-17; 19:5-6; *Heb* 6:2). Just as we can differentiate the moment of Easter from Pentecost, so also in the life of the Christian who is inserted in the sacramental economy there are two distinct and interconnected moments: baptism, which accentuates the Easter configuration, and confirmation, which refers more directly to

---

[108] Cf. Congregation for the Doctrine of the Faith, Instruction *Pastoralis actio*, 15 and 28, no. 2: AAS 72 (1980), 1144-1145 and 1151.

Pentecost, with the reception of the Spirit, to full incorporation into the ecclesial mission. In the Christian initiation of adults both aspects take place in a single joint celebration.

96. [*Historical Foundation*]. Since ancient times, a series of post-baptismal rites have been recognised, not always clearly distinguished from baptism itself, such as the laying on of hands, the anointing with the chrism oil and the signing with the sign of the cross.[109] The Church has always maintained that these post-baptismal rites were part of complete Christian initiation. With the passing of history and the increase of Christians, the East maintained the consecutive unity of baptism, chrismation and first Eucharist, given by the priest, although only the bishop is responsible for the blessing of oil. In the West, however, the anointing with the oil of chrism was reserved for the bishop[110] and, for centuries, until an intervention by Pius X in 1910,[111] took place during the bishop's visit, before First Communion. Already at the beginning of the fourth century, in the Council of Elvira (ca. 302), the difference and the distance in time between baptism and confirmation is recognised.[112]

b) Faith and Confirmation

97. In the ritual of Confirmation, the renunciations are renewed and the profession of baptismal faith is repeated. This marks their continuity with baptism as well as the need for its precedence. The characteristic of Confirmation resides in a double element related to faith. In the first place, a fuller adherence and a "special strength" of the Holy Spirit (LG 11), as the same rite points out: "N., by this sign receive the Gift of the Holy Spirit."[113] Secondly,

---

[109] Cf. *Traditio apostolica*, 22 (SCh 11, 52-53).

[110] Cf. Innocent I, *Letter to Decentius*, Bishop of Gubbio (year 416; DH 215).

[111] *Decree of the Sacred Congregation of the Discipline of the Sacraments on First Communion "Quam singulari"* (8th August 1910): AAS 2 (1910) 582ff (DH 3530ff).

[112] Council of Elvira, canon 77 (DH 121; G. Martinez Diaz- Fr. Rodriguez, *Colección canónica hispana*, vol. IV, Madrid 1984, 267).

[113] *Rite of Confirmation*. Cf. *Catechism of the Catholic Church*, 1294-1296.

Confirmation implies a "closer bond with the Church" (LG 11). Thus, the ecclesiality of faith is reaffirmed. Consequently, baptismal faith is strengthened in several directions. It is a faith more disposed to the public witness of the ecclesial faith; it is a faith with greater vigour and ecclesial identification; it is a more active faith, inasmuch as it is more conformed by the gift of the Spirit, subsequent to the first baptismal reception of the Spirit. These aspects denote a maturing of faith compared to the initial faith required for baptism. Without these dispositions of faith, the sacrament is in danger of remaining in an empty rite.

98. The presence of the bishop, the "original" minister of Confirmation (LG 26), expresses emphatically the ecclesial nature of Confirmation. To the union with the Holy Spirit is added the union with the Church. Participation in Confirmation is the sign and means of ecclesial communion. Confirmation celebrated by the local bishop promotes spiritual unity between the bishop and the local Church. The confirmed one is incorporated into the Church, contributing to the building of the body of Christ (cf. *Eph* 4:12; *1 Cor* 12). In addition, it strengthens his Christian life, already begun with baptism. Through the new gift of the Spirit he is better equipped to be a living witness of the faith received, like what happened at Pentecost.

c) Current Problems

99. The present location of the sacrament of Confirmation in the West is due more to historical and pastoral circumstances than to properly theological reasons or reasons derived from the specificity of the sacrament. In Christian initiation of adults, the original and theologically more consistent rhythm is maintained: Baptism, Confirmation, and the Eucharist. Although the sacrament of Confirmation offers the possibility of continuing instruction in the faith, insertion into the Church and the personalisation of the decision that the parents and godparents took in their day in favour of the child, it cannot be expected to solve the difficulties of youth ministry nor the disaffection of the

74

young people who were baptised at the time with regard to the ecclesial institution and the faith. Despite praiseworthy efforts and the fact that at times it implies a more mature rediscovery of the faith, with the passage to a more conscious and adult active belonging, in not few occasions young people experience the celebration of Confirmation as a sort of university graduation: once the degree has been obtained, there is no need to return to the classroom. Others simply understand Confirmation as a condition for further steps, such as marriage, without grasping what is proper to this sacrament, blurred in the feelings of many faithful.

d) Pastoral Proposal: Faith for Confirmation

100. The importance of baptism has been held firm with much constancy, as has its theological profile. The postponement of Confirmation, where it is deferred for a long time, or even not administered, has made it difficult to appreciate its place in Christian initiation, as a sacrament of the Spirit and of the Church, fundamental elements in Christian initiation. A missionary Church is made up of confirmed Christians who, in the power of the Spirit, take full responsibility for their faith. A Christian logically wants to be the sacrament of Christ. That is why he is fully incorporated into the Church and asks for the gift of the Spirit through the Chrism and the laying on of hands, if it was not received together with baptism. Just as Christ received the anointing of the Spirit as he came out of the waters, so the Christian who is configured to Christ also accomplishes his journey of faith in the Spirit, strengthened by Confirmation.[114]

101. In adult Christian initiation, the faith required for Confirmation coincides with that necessary for baptism. In the case of deferred reception of both sacraments, baptismal faith will have matured in several directions. Progress will have been made in the personal appropriation of the ecclesial faith and

---

[114] *Catechism of the Catholic Church*, 1285, 1294.

in the sense of belonging. This implies a better knowledge, a greater capacity to give an account of the ecclesial faith and an adequate conformation of life with it. There will also be a path of personal relationship with the Trinitarian God, in particular through prayer. More decisively, faith will have shaped the biography, having made a journey of following Christ in the Church. Confirmation implies the desire and decision to continue on this path, finding, through the discernment made possible by the Spirit, the proper way to follow Jesus and witness to him. The key to this is a deep personal relationship with the Lord gained through prayer, which leads to witness, ecclesial belonging and assiduous sacramental practise. Just as the sacramental economy does not close with Easter, but includes Pentecost, so Christian initiation is not closed with baptism. If there was a phase of waiting and preparation for the reception of the gift of the Spirit, presided over by prayer (cf. *Acts* 1:14), so also the adequate catechesis for the reception of Confirmation, without forgetting the other elements – doctrine, morals, offers the opportunity for an intensification and personalisation of the relationship with the Lord through prayer.

3.3. RECIPROCITY BETWEEN FAITH AND THE EUCHARIST

a) Biblical Foundation

102. What happened at the Last Supper (*Mt* 26:26-29; *Mk* 14:22-26; *Lk* 22:14-23; *1 Cor* 11:23-26) has always been considered the institution of the Eucharist. To these fundamental stories must be added others in which the Church has seen a Eucharistic tenor: the multiplication of the loaves (*Mk* 6:30-44 and similar; 8:1-10 and similar; *Jn* 6:1-14); Paul's admonitions to the community of Corinth (*1 Cor* 10-11); or the episode that closes the meeting of Emmaus with the Risen One (*Lk* 24:30-31; 35). Following the force of the command "do this in memory of me" (*1 Cor* 11:24, cf. 25; *Lk* 22:19), from the beginning (e.g., *Acts* 2:42, 46; 20:7; 27:35) until today, where there are Christians and the Church,

the Eucharist is celebrated, which is the memorial of the Passion and Resurrection of the Lord until he returns, his saving gift for "many," for all (cf. *Rom* 5:18-19; 8:32).

103. At the Last Supper, the Lord Jesus condenses the meaning of his whole life, of his impending death and of his future resurrection to hand it down to his disciples as a memorial and an eminent sign of his love. For this reason, what happened there and the sacramental remembrance of his Passion and Resurrection display an extraordinary density. In the Eucharist, the Church celebrates the making present and actualisation of Christ's gift of his sacrifice for all of us to the Father. In the Eucharist, thanksgiving to the Father "through Christ, with him and in him"[115] made present by the action of the Spirit, the Church unites herself to Christ, associates herself with him, and becomes his Body. For this reason, it has been possible to affirm with truth that the Church is born of the Eucharist.[116] Since the Eucharist gathers the very essence of the life of Christ and, therefore, of the Christian life, it is both the source and the summit of the Christian life (SC 10; LG 11).

b) Faith and the Eucharist

104. [*Trinitarian Faith*]. Each Eucharist beings "in the name of the Father and of the Son and of the Holy Spirit": with a reminder of the baptismal formula, and of the Trinitarian Creed which runs through and permeates the whole celebration. "The first element of Eucharistic faith is the mystery of God himself, Trinitarian love."[117] For in the Eucharist, we enter into communion of life with the love of the Trinitarian God. As the greatest sign of his love, the Father gave his Son for our salvation, who in turn

---

[115] Doxology that concludes the Eucharistic Prayer. See for example, *Roman Missal*, 3rd Editio Typica, §§ 119, 127, 136, 144.

[116] Cf. St John Paul II, Encyclical *Ecclesia de Eucharistia* (17th April 2003) spec. 1 and 21-25: AAS 95 (2003), 433-434 and 447-450.

[117] Benedict XVI, Apostolic Exhortation *Sacramentum caritatis* (22nd February 2007) 7: AAS 99 (2007), 110.

offered himself in "the power of the eternal Spirit" (*Heb* 9:14). In the Eucharist, we are made partakers of this loving current, inherent in divine intimacy. To the Trinitarian God, we present the best possible praise through Christ in the unity of the Spirit, as solemnly proclaimed by the doxology with which the Eucharistic prayer culminates. Thanksgiving to the Father through the Son given for us and through the gift of the Spirit is marked by the praise which involves personal witness in ordinary life.

105. [*Unity of Faith and Charity*]. The penitential act, situated at the beginning of the Eucharist celebration, manifests the need of every sincere believer to receive the forgiveness of sins, to be reconciled with God and with his brothers and sisters, in order to be able to enter into communion with God. Furthermore, the penitential act underlines the inseparability between the vertical communion with Christ, whose surrender will be remembered immediately (*anamnesis*), and the horizontal communion with other Christians and, beyond it, with all men. True Eucharistic faith is always an active faith through charity (cf. *Gal* 5:6). In the Eucharist: "love of God and love of neighbour are truly united: the incarnate God draws us all to himself. We thus understand how *agape* also became a term for the Eucharist: there God's own *agape* comes to us bodily, in order to continue his work in us and through us."[118]

106. [*Faith as a Response to the Word of God*]. Since the eleventh century, the same Creed with which the baptismal rite concludes has been a fixed part of the Eucharist celebration on Sundays and solemnities. This confession of faith is simultaneously a response to the Word of God and an expression of unity among believers. Through faith in the proclamation of the Word, we

---

[118] Benedict XVI, Encyclical Letter *Deus caritas est* (25th December 2006) 14 : AAS 98 (2006), 229. Cf. Benedict XVI, Apostolic Exhortation *Sacramentum caritatis* (22nd February 2007) spec. 88-89: AAS 99 (2007), 172-174.

hear the voice of Christ.[119] The prophetic dimension of faith also emerges. A powerful Word, capable of transforming the world, just as it happens in the heart of the Eucharistic celebration with the gifts that are presented and the assembly that celebrates. Thus begins the eschatological transformation of which the Church, the body of Christ, is a foretaste.

107. [*Pneumatic Dimension of Faith*]. The pneumatic nature of the sacraments appears with meridian clarity in the Eucharistic celebration. In the current Latin rite, there is a double *epiclesis*. The first is over the gifts, which will be transformed into the given body and shed blood of Jesus Christ. The second is over the assembly, which in turn also becomes the body of Christ, entering into living communion with all the saints. This communion is already seen in the solemn song of the *Sanctus*, in which the voices of heaven and earth unite in common praise. Therefore, in the Eucharistic liturgy we take part in the heavenly liturgy (cf. SC 8). Consequently, the pneumatic dimension of ecclesial faith comes into play in a substantive way in the Eucharist and illuminates the power that the Spirit possesses to transform both the believer and the worldly reality, to elevate them and lead them to divine communion and praise.

108. [*Faith as devotion to Mystery*]. After the words of the consecration, the celebrant proclaims: "Mysterium fidei"[120] (the mystery of faith). This solemn acclamation is, at the same time, an affirmation, an announcement and an invitation addressed to all. To such an extent the Eucharist is a mystery of faith, which without faith can neither be understood nor celebrated. The acclamation manifests that the sacramental truth of what is celebrated, that the species of bread and wine have become the

---

[119] "When the Sacred Scriptures are read in the Church, God himself speaks to his people, and Christ, present in his own word, proclaims the Gospel" (*General Instruction of the Roman Missal*, 29).

[120] Roman Canon, in the *Roman Missal*, 3rd Editio Typica, § 112. See the commentary of Benedict XVI, Apostolic Exhortation *Sacramentum caritatis* (22nd February 2007) 6: AAS 99 (2007), 109-110.

Body and Blood of Christ, is really a mystery of faith. Just as the eyes of faith perceived in Jesus of Nazareth the Messiah of God, so those same eyes now perceive the sacramental presence of Jesus Christ.[121] The mystery of Christ is known through revelation (cf. *1 Cor* 2:7-11; *Col* 1: 26-27; 2:2; *Eph* 1:9; 3:3, 9) and faith.

109. [*Faith as Recognition of the Sacramental Economy*]. In the recitation of the solemn Eucharistic Prayer, the great milestones of the sacramental economy are recalled in thanksgiving and supplication: from creation to final eschatological consummation. In particular, we remember the gift of the Lord Jesus on the Cross, his resurrection and the meaning that the Lord himself gave to his redemptive death in the context of the Last Supper. Faith in the divine economy as a whole is trained and strengthened in the Eucharistic liturgy.

110. [*Eschatological Dimension of Faith*]. In the sacramental celebration of the mystery, the past, the memory of what happened, the present, the making present or actualisation of what happened, and the future, which is anticipation of the final fulness what we await, come together.[122] The eschatological novelty initiated by the Word through his incarnation, life, death and resurrection has already begun to be realised in the christification of the assembly and of the world that takes place in the Eucharist.

111. [*Faith and Communion with Christ*]. Communion, as its name indicates, expresses an intimate union with Christ,

---

[121] Cf. St Thomas Aquinas, *ST* III, q. 76, a.7. The well-known hymn, Adoro Te Devote, expresses magnificently what we say. Here is an example: "In cruce latebat sola Deitas, At hic latet simul et humanitas; Ambo tamen credens atque confitens, Peto quod petivit latro poenitens" (*Rituale Romanum de sacra communion et de cultu mysterii eucharistici extra missam*, Vatican City 1973, § 198, pp. 61-62).

[122] Francis, Encyclical Letter *Lumen fidei* (29th June 2013) 44 : AAS 105 (2013), 584-585. A famous antiphon describes it splendidly: "O sacrum convivium in quo Christus sumitur: recolitur memoria passionis eius: mens impletur gratia: et futurae nobis pignus datur" ("Ad Magnificat, antifona. Ad II Vesperas Sanctissimi Corporis et Sanguinis Christi," In *Liturgia Horarum iuxta ritum romanum*, vol. III, Tempus per annum. *Hebdomadae* I-XVII, Vatican City 2000, 54).

through the Spirit, which is impossible without faith. One cannot commune intimately with someone by ignoring them or against one's will. The faith that responds with the word "amen" to the Eucharistic gifts is related to the disposition not only to receive the sacrament, but to represent it. With this communion with Christ comes the personal sanctification of the Christian, concomitant with the communion of life with Christ. This sanctification necessarily implies a sending.

112. [*Missionary Character of Faith*]. The final sending with which the Eucharist ends, "Ite, missa est,"[123] supposes a missionary return to ordinary life, to make present in it the life received in the sacrament, and to become a Eucharist for the world in the likeness of Christ and in his own way. In fact, in the Eucharistic offering, not only does Jesus Christ offer himself, but every believer who participates in the Eucharist also offers himself together with Christ (cf. SC 48; LG 11; *Rom* 12:1). The personal offering, the acceptance of being sent and its exercise cannot take place without faith. Everything that the faithful Christian receives in the sacrament: the forgiveness of venial sins, the renewal of baptism, the preaching of the Word, communion with Christ and transformation into the body of Christ through the Holy Spirit, implies a strengthening that enables him now, Christianised, to witness faith in the world and to transform reality according to God's plan. Thus, after the event of the reception of the gift of the Father, by the gift of the Son received in the Spirit, which takes place in every Eucharist, the Christian is expressly sent on mission at the end of the celebration.

113. [*Strengthening Personal Faith*]. The faith of the believer is enriched and strengthened by intimate communion with Christ. The ecclesial being of the one who participates in the Eucharist, its insertion into the visible body of Christ, is actualised and intensified. Incorporation into Christ is of such calibre that

---

[123] *Roman Missal*, Concluding Rites. It can be found in *Appendix Missalis Romani*, Madrid 2017, § 96 (p. 50).

Augustine says to the faithful: "If you are members of the body of Christ, your mystery rests on the table of the Lord.... be what you see, and receive what you are."[124] In short, in faith we recognise that the Eucharist supposes the most intense way of Christ's presence among us, since it is a real, corporeal and substantial presence.[125] For this very reason, full participation in the Eucharist from the point of view of faith implies maximum communion with Christ.

114. [*Building the Ecclesial Body*]. In the Eucharist not only is the individual faith of the believer strengthened, but in it the Church is generated[126]: Christ, who gives himself to her in sacrifice as to his beloved Spouse, constitutes her in his body.[127] Communion among the Churches, the sharing of the same faith received, is expressed through Eucharistic communion following a very ancient tradition. The Church of her own is the body of Christ, constituted as such by divine design, thanks to the sacramental Trinitarian action. This body realises what it is when it proclaims the faith received, sanctifies history, sings the praises of the Trinity and commits itself in mission to the proclamation of the Gospel in word and deed.

115. [*The Eucharist: Greatest Expression of Sacramental Faith*]. We can therefore conclude by affirming that: "The sacramental character of faith finds its highest expression in the Eucharist. The Eucharist is a precious nourishment for faith: an encounter with Christ truly present in the supreme act of his love, the life-giving gift of himself."[128]

---

[124] "Si ergo vos estis corpus Christi et membra, mysterium vestrum in mensa Dominica positum est [...] Estote quod videtis, et accipite quod estis" (Augustine, *Sermo* 272; PL 38, 1247ff).

[125] St Paul VI, Encyclical Letter *Mysterium fidei* (3rd September 1965) 5: AAS 57 (1965), 764.

[126] Cf. St John Paul II, Encyclical Letter *Ecclesia de Eucharistia*, *passim* (17th April 2003): AAS 95 (2003), 433-475.

[127] Cf. Benedict XVI, Apostolic Exhortation *Sacramentum caritatis* (22nd February 2007) 14 and 27: AAS 99 (2007), 115-116 and 127.

[128] Francis, Encyclical Letter *Lumen fidei* (29th June 2013) 44 : AAS 105 (2013), 584.

116. [*Necessity of Faith for participation in the Eucharistic celebration*]. Paul's admonition to the Christians at Corinth is especially instructive. He who is involved in idolatrous behavior cannot partake of the Body or Blood of Christ (*1 Cor* 10:14-22). Communion with "the table of the Lord" requires not only to have been initiated into the Christian faith and to be a member of the Body of Christ, but also a consistency of life with what is meant there. In the same way, a conduct as inconsistent with the Christian faith as divisions in the community and the notable lack of charity towards the brethren (*1 Cor* 11:21) is incompatible with "eating the Lord's Supper" (*1 Cor* 11:20). This obliges us to discern whether or not we are living in a fundamental line of conformity with what is being celebrated (*1 Cor* 11:29). In short, Eucharistic participation requires a living faith, which is manifested through charity and the abandonment of idols. Eucharistic praxis requires both the exercise of charity, as well as doctrinal conformity and ecclesial insertion.

117. The penitential institution of the ancient Church excluded for a time from Eucharistic communion (not from the Church) members of the faithful who had publicly renounced their faith, or who had violated the Creed and the rules of life prescribed by the Church. After a public confession, the sinner, turned into an occasion of public scandal, was expelled from Eucharistic communion for a time (excommunication), and later he was received again solemnly after having fulfilled the penance (reconciliation). Thus it became visible that penance was not only used for the reconciliation of the sinner with Christ, but also for the purification of the Church. The penitent understands himself as the stone of a Church that is to be the light of the world. When it ceased to be so because of a public sin, it became necessary in a certain way to remove it (excommunication), to "repair it" it through penance and to put it back in place (reconciliation).[129] Despite the change in the way penance is celebrated, which is no longer public, the basic theology has not changed. However, nowadays

---

[129] Cf. *The Shepherd of Hermas*, Comp. IX (Funk, 211 and ff).

this close correlation between penance and the Eucharist has become blurred in many practising environments.

c) Current Problems

118. Many of those who consider themselves Catholics believe that regular Sunday Eucharistic attendance is excessive. Others maintain the practise of frequent communion or whenever they attend Mass, without ever going to the sacrament of confession. Not a few take the Eucharist as a personal devotion, freely available to them according to their own needs or feelings. During great liturgical feasts, especially Christmas, Easter or some great local feasts, as well as in some unique celebrations (such as weddings and funerals), there are some unusual members of the faithful who come to participate in the Eucharist, including taking Holy Communion, without any qualms of conscience; and then they disappear until the following year or the following exceptional occasion. These practises, though theologically inconsistent, reflect the persistent influence of the Christian faith in the life of non-practising or distant people. This remainder of Christian influence, albeit with deviations, can be a starting point for a more conscious ecclesial reintegration and offers the possibility of reviving a lifeless faith. However, they also show, in their ambivalence, how in many ways there is a gap between what the Church believes to celebrate in the Eucharist, the requirements for full participation in the Eucharist, the consequences it entails in ordinary life, and what many believers seek in occasional or sporadic celebrations of the Eucharist.

d) Lights from the Tradition

119. The conditions for the reception of the Eucharist have been established since the earliest times. As we have indicated, Paul warns those who approach the Eucharist: "For anyone who eats and drinks without discerning the body, eats and drinks condemnation upon himself" (*1 Cor* 11:29), highlighting some indispensable requirements. From the Gospel of John,

it can be inferred that a reception of the sacramental species without faith that is without Spirit does not profit at all, because it requires faith (cf. *Jn* 6:63-69). Justin Martyr mentions the following as necessary requirements: belief that the gifts are what they signify; the receiver must be baptised, and must not deny the doctrine of Christ through his life.[130] The recently quoted Pauline exhortation resounds again in the Didache: "If anyone is a saint, let him come; if anyone is not a saint, let him be converted!",[131] and in a similar way in the *Apostolic Constitutions.*[132] It is reflected in the liturgical invitation "the holy to the saints"[133] that was already commented by Theodore of Mopsuestia. With the "saints" refers, first of all, as Paul did, to the baptised, those who live with the Church. This thinking is manifested both in the homilies of John Chrysostom[134] and in Cyprian: communion with Christ cannot be dissociated from communion with the Church.[135] The doctor of the Eucharist demands that his priests, if necessary, reject some people.[136] Augustine, too, with equal clarity, warns that sacramental food produces salvific effect and life only when it is eaten "spiritually," with faith in its invisible content and with an upright conscience.[137] That is to say, with a life that corresponds to the love of Christ and his members.

---

[130] *1st Apol.* 66ff (Wartelle, 190ff).

[131] *Didache*, 10, 6; 9,5 (Funk 6;5).

[132] *Apostolic Constitutions*, VII, 26, 6 (SCh 336, 57): "If one is a saint, let him draw near; but whoever is not, let him become one through penance."

[133] Present in: the Liturgy of Saint John Chrysostom (67); Liturgy of St Basil (131); Liturgy of the Presanctified Gifts (168). The pages refer to: *Liturgikon. The Divine Liturgy of Saint John Chrysostom, of Saint Basil, of the Presanctified Gifts* (Madrid, 2016).

[134] John Chrysostom, *Hom. in Matth.* 82, 4 (PG 58, 743): faith in the real presence; *hom.* 25, 3 (PG 57, 330ff); *hom.* 7,6 (PG 57, 79ff). *Super Rom. hom.* 8 (9), 8(PG 60, 464-466): Love of neighbour. *Super Hebr.* 17, 4-5 (PG 63, 131-134).

[135] Cyprian, *Epistula* 57, 2 (CSEL 3/2, 651-652).

[136] John Chrysostom, *In Matth. hom.* 82, 5. 6 (PG 58, 743-746): responsibility of the priest in the administration.

[137] Augustine, *In Iohannis ev.*, XXVI, 11 (CCSL 36, 264ff).

120. Scholastic theology calls this disposition "formed faith" (*fides formata*), a faith shaped by love[138](cf.§§ 62-64). In this sense, St Thomas Aquinas distinguishes the following: the content of this sacrament can only be received in faith, since it is a "sacrament of faith" (*mysterium fidei*).[139] "Infidelity" (*infidelitas*) makes one inept in eminent degree for the reception of the sacrament, since unbelief "separates from the unity of the Church"[140]; unity that the Eucharist signifies. In certain circumstances, however, when one "wants to receive what the Church gives," in that case one receives the sacrament, even though his faith is deficient in its contents.[141] Someone who believes in the presence of Christ in the Eucharist, but is not in a state of grace, receives the sacrament, but commits a grave sin.[142] St Thomas argues that a lie has been committed (*falsitas*): what the sacrament expresses, the love that unites Christ with his faithful, does not happen in the recipient.[143] St Thomas realises that a fruitful participation in baptism and the Eucharist requires in each case *a different degree of disposition generated by faith*. For baptism, the intention of receiving what the Church gives is sufficient. In Holy Communion, however, it is necessary to understand the sacrament as such and to believe.[144]

---

[138] St Thomas Aquinas, *ST* III, q.80, a.4.

[139] Cf. also Bonaventure, IV *Sent*. dist. 9 a.1 qq.1-4: sacramentaliter, spiritualiter manducare.

[140] St Thomas Aquinas, *ST* III, q.80, a.5, ad 2.

[141] "si infidelis sumat species sacramentales, corpus Christi sub sacramento sumit. Unde manducat Christum sacramentaliter, si ly "sacramentaliter" determinat verbum ex parte manducati. Si autem ex parte manducantis, tunc proprie loquendo non manducat sacramentaliter; quia non utitur eo quod accipit ut sacramento, sed ut simplici cibo. Nisi forte infidelis *intenderet recipere* illud quod Ecclesia confert, licet non haberet fidem veram circa alios articulos vel etiam hoc sacramentum" (St Thomas Aquinas, *ST* III, q.80, a.3, ad 2; emphasis ours).

[142] Cf. *ST* III, q.79, a.3.

[143] "Quicumque ergo hoc sacramentum sumit, ex hoc ipso significat, se esse Christo unitum et membris eius incorporatum. Quod quidem fit per fidem formatam" (*ST* III, q.80, a.4).

[144] St Thomas Aquinas, *Sent*. IV dist. 9 q.1, a.2, q.2, ad 2; cf. *ST* III, q.79, a.7,ad 2; a.8, ad 2 (The latter on the difference between Baptism and the Eucharist).

121. In the liturgical traditions, particularly in the East, this interconnection between faith, love and the reception of the Eucharist is clearly perceived. For example, in the convocation to the communion of the people, it says: "Draw near with faith, charity and fear of God."[145] In the liturgy of St John Chrysostom and in the liturgy of St Basil, the deacon, the priest, and the people recite a confession of Christological faith expressed before Christ, present in Body and Blood, just before receiving Holy Communion. He says: "I believe, Lord, and confess that you are Christ, the Son of the living God, who came into the world to save sinners. I also believe that this is your immaculate Body and this is your Precious Blood."[146] The Syriac tradition, witnessed by Ephrem, understands that the promises linked to the two trees of Eden (*Gn* 2:17; 3:2) are to be truly fulfilled. The initial error in eating the "tree of the knowledge of good and evil" produced a fall, which had to be straightened out. Eating from the "tree of life" becomes a reality in Eucharistic communion with the Eucharistic offering of Christ on the tree of the Cross.[147] In the Eucharistic celebration, the liturgy of the Word becomes a fruitful and corrective eating of the "tree of knowledge of good and evil." After that suitable meal, all are invited to eat from the "tree of life" in Eucharistic Communion.

e) Pastoral Proposal: Faith for the Eucharist

122. Baptism is the beginning of a pilgrimage, the culmination of which is only reached at the *Eschaton*. For this reason, Christians receive again and again the sacrament of the Eucharist, which is food for the journey. For this reason, the Church has never ceased to gather together to celebrate the mystery of the Passover, to read in this context "that which refers to him in all the Scriptures" (*Lk* 24:27) and to celebrate the banquet at which the self-giving

---

[145] *Liturgikon*, 73.

[146] *Liturgy of St John Chrysostom* (*Liturgikon*, 69-73); *Liturgy of St Basil* (*Ibid.*, 133-135). In a similar way the Coptic liturgy: *Die koptische Liturgie*, übers. und kommentiert von KARAM KHELLA, [1989], 186.

[147] *In Genesim*, II, 23 (CSCO 152, 39; 153, 29-30).

of the crucified and risen Saviour is transmitted in the present of believers. However, one cannot receive adequately the gift that the existential sacrifice of Christ implies if one is not willing to allow oneself to be configured existentially by this gift in faith. Without faith, neither Pilate nor the Roman soldiers nor the people understood how in the death on the Cross of Jesus Christ, God was reconciling the world to himself (*2 Cor* 5:19); without faith it is not perceived that he who hung on the tree is the Son of God (*Mk* 15:39). The believing gaze sees not only blood and water coming from the pierced side, but also the Church, founded on baptism and the Eucharist (cf. *Jn* 19:34). The blood and water that flow from there is the source and the power of the Church.[148] The Son of God truly becomes "Emmanuel" in every Christian through participation in the Body and Blood of Christ.[149]

123. [*Sacramental Faith and the Eucharist*]. Without sacramental faith, participation in the Eucharist, especially receiving Holy Communion, is meaningless. The Eucharist does not refer to an undifferentiated or generic relationship with divinity. The sacramental faith that intervenes in the celebration of the Eucharist is a Trinitarian faith. In the Eucharist we profess a living relationship with the Trinitarian God. We thank the Father for the gift of salvation we received. The gift of salvation was actualised through the gift of his Son in the power of the Spirit, which is now recalled and made present in the celebration.

124. Sacramental faith presupposes that such an action of the Trinity is recognised, and that the Eucharistic banquet is perceived as an authentic anticipation of the future eschatological banquet. The power of God is already breaking in, transforming and sanctifying believers, making them fellow citizens with the saints (*Eph* 2:19) and citizens of the heavenly Jerusalem (cf. *Heb* 12:22; cf. *Rev* 21-22; *Heb* 11:13).

---

[148] Ephrem, *Commentary on the Diatessaron*, XXI, 11 (CSCO 137, 145; 145, 227-228).
[149] Ephrem, *De virginitate*, 37, 2 (CSCO 223, 133).

125. Sacramental faith is expressed, moreover, in the irrevocable self-attachment of Jesus Christ to the sacrament (*ex opere operato*) with the species of consecrated bread and wine through the invocation of the Spirit in the *epiclesis*, with the result that the recipient not only can hope, but knows in faith that at a given moment he receives what the consecrated species signify.

126. Sacramental faith also implies the sacramentalisation of the recipient himself. He not only receives a sacrament, he himself becomes in a certain sense a "sacrament," in the sense that an intense conformation to Christ has been brought about by the action of the Spirit; and he now lives in close union with Christ and the Church, which empowers him to offer himself to God as a living and spiritual sacrifice (cf. *Rom* 12:1) and to bear witness to the Christian life. Said with images, he is transformed into a living stone of the confessing community, of which Vatican II says it is Christ's means and instrument to bring all men to his home.

127. [*Sacramental Faith and Ecclesial Communion in the Eucharist*]. From this point of view, the individual realisation of personal faith cannot be separated from the faith of the community celebrating the sacrament. There is unity and continuity between what is celebrated (*lex orandi*), what is believed (*lex credendi*), and what is lived (*lex vivendi*), in the framework of which flows Christian life, personal prayer and sacramental celebration. Since the truth that Christians profess is a person, Jesus Christ, it must also be represented personally by the apostles and their successors. The Eucharistic communion with Christ of each individual is to be verified through the communion of faith with the Pope and the local bishop, mentioned by name in each Eucharistic celebration. He who receives Holy Communion does not confess Christ alone, but also communes with the confession of faith of the community in which he participates in the Eucharist.

128. Translated into other categories, this means a clear and conscious adherence to the faith of the Church, which explicitly includes the following: Trinitarian faith embodied in the Creed; the Christological faith concentrated on the redemptive meaning of the death of Christ, the Son of God, the Lord, "for many" and "for me," and of resurrection; the pneumatological faith, particularly active and present through the double *epiclesis*, which is fundamental in the celebration; and faith in what the Eucharist signifies as sacrament of the body of Christ and of the ecclesial body. All of this is framed in a believing itinerary, which aspires, trusting in the powerful force of the Spirit and his permanent help, to conform one's life to the mystery of Christ and to witness to it with joy in the midst of the vicissitudes of life. On this journey, Christians often turn to Eucharistic food, to receive the gift of communion with Christ, in order to continue to grow in faith, hope and love until eternal life.

129. [*Inconsistency of Eucharistic Participation without Faith in what it Celebrates*]. Full participation in the Eucharist means communion with the body of Christ (cf. LG 3) and the Church. It does not seem possible to approach it with consistency if: one does not recognise what the sacramental presence of Christ means in the Eucharist; one rejects the Trinitarian faith of the Church, invoked at various times during the celebration, sealed with the recitation of the Creed; Christian charity suffers serious deficiencies in one's personal life; any conscious and deliberate act has been committed in a matter that seriously compromises what faith and ecclesial morals say (mortal sin[150]).

130. [*Ways of Growing*]. Whoever is on a journey with Christ goes to the Sunday Eucharist not because it is an obligation established by the Church, but from the desire to be strengthened by the loving mercy of the Lord. This desire includes readiness for necessary sacramental reconciliation with Christ and the Church, when needed. Now, even without the emotional pressure

---

[150] Cf. *Catechism of the Catholic Church*, 1855-1861.

of desire, those who participate in the Catholic faith know that they have joined a community with a sacramental structure. For this reason he is also aware that his sacramental participation and, concretely, the Eucharist is part of the public witness to which he has freely committed himself. He commits himself to testify to the sacramental reality of faith, in order to make clear the visibility of grace and thus strengthen the sacramentality of the Church, his community of belonging.

131. Because of the reciprocal causality that exists between faith and the Eucharist, in areas where there was not or there is not usually a celebration of Mass and sacramental catechesis, due to the limits of the ecclesial institution, it becomes more difficult to discover the meaning of the Sunday Eucharistic praxis. At the same time, the lack of frequent participation at the table of the Word of God and the Body of Christ, through personal or pastoral failures, is a lack that hinders growth toward a fuller sacramental faith. In addition to taking care of Eucharistic celebrations at all their ends, in accordance with their meaning, it is appropriate to propose ways of reintegration into the ecclesial faith, when it has been lost, that culminate in the Eucharist as the crowning of this return; and it is appropriate to propose other types of non-Eucharistic celebrations and spaces of encounter, prayer and extended Christian catechesis for people whose evangelisation has not yet matured to participate consciously in the Eucharist.

4. THE RECIPROCITY BETWEEN FAITH AND MARRIAGE

132. [*Problem*]. If there is one sacrament in which the essential reciprocity between faith and sacraments is put to the test, it is marriage for various reasons. In the very definition of the sacrament of marriage, according to the Latin Church, faith does not appear explicitly (cf. § 143). It is presupposed, so to speak, by the prior act of baptism, the sacrament of faith par excellence. Furthermore, for the validity of marriage between baptised persons in the Latin Church, the intention to celebrate a sacrament is not required[151]; it is not required to have the desire or awareness of the sacramentality of the marriage union, but only the intention to contract a natural marriage, this means according to the creatural order, with the properties that the Church considers inherent in natural marriage. Within this understanding of marriage it is incumbent upon theology to elucidate the complex case of marriages between "baptised non-believers." An outright defence of the sacramentality of such unions would undermine the essential reciprocity between faith and sacraments, as proper to the sacramental economy, supporting, at least in the case of marriage, a sacramental automatism which we have been rejecting as unworthy of the Christian faith (cf. *supra* chap. 2).

133. [*Approach*]. Aware of the difficulty of the question posed under the heading "reciprocity between faith and marriage," we shall proceed as follows. First, since, even if we share a common stem, there are notable differences in the theology of marriage between the Latin and Eastern traditions, we focus exclusively on the Latin understanding. The rich Eastern tradition has its own physiognomy. We point out some distinctive aspects between the two. While in Latin theology the predominant understanding

---

[151] Cf. CIC, canon 1099.

is that the spouses are the ministers of the sacrament and that the sacrament takes places through the free mutual consent of the spouses, for the Eastern tradition the blessing of the bishop or priest belongs in its own right to the essence of the sacrament.[152] Only the sacred minister has been given the faculty to invoke the Spirit (*epiclesis*) to accomplish the sanctification inherent in the sacrament. It has its own complete canonical regulation.[153] This is due to a conception of the sacrament of marriage which springs from a theology with its own personality and profile, in which the sanctifying effects of the sacrament are put in the foreground.[154]

134. Second, we treat, according to the usual methodology (cf. § 80), with its adaptations, the ordinary case of the sacrament of marriage. Next we investigate the doubtful question about the sacramental quality of marriages between "baptised non-believers," in a twofold approach. First we look at the state of the question and then we offer a theological proposal for a solution, congruent with the reciprocity between faith and sacraments, which does not deny the current theology of marriage.

4.1. THE SACRAMENT OF MARRIAGE

a) Biblical Foundation

135. [*Marriage in the Divine Plan*]. Although each sacrament has its own specific singularity, the case of marriage stands out because of its particularity. Marriage as such belongs to the creatural order, within the divine plan (cf. GS 48). The creatural reality of marriage rests on the relational capacity between people of different sex, male and female (*Gn* 1:27), closely linked to fertility (*Gn* 1:28), which culminates in such a form of union

---

[152] Cf. CCEO, canon 828.

[153] Cf. CCEO, *Titulus XVI: De cultu divino et praesertim de sacramentis. Caput VII : De matrimonio*, canons 776-866.

[154] "Ex Christi institutione matrimonium validum inter baptizatos eo ipso est sacramentum, quo coniuges ad imaginem indefectibilis unionis Christi cum Ecclesia a Deo uniuntur gratiaque sacramentali veluti consecrantur et roborantur" (CCEO, canon 776, § 2).

that they form "one flesh" (cf. *Gn* 2:23-24). God's sacramental interlocution throughout the divine economy of salvation finds here a reality, created by God in his image, in the image of the Trinitarian God,[155] very capable of expressing by itself the loving, covenantal relationship between God and the people, his wife, always symbolically represented by a woman. In the Christian perspective, this creatural reality becomes a sacrament, that is, a visible sign of Christ's love for the Church (*Eph* 5:25, 31-32).

136. [*Marriage in the Teachings of Jesus*]. Faced with the practise of repudiation (*Dt* 22:19, 29; 24:1-4), Jesus reiterates God's original plan: "What God has joined together, no man must separate" (*Mk* 10:9 and *Mt* 19:6; cf. *Gn* 2:24; *1 Cor* 6:16), clarifying that divorce was a concession due to hardness of heart (*Mk* 10:5 and *Mt* 19:8). Throughout history, the interpretation of the Matthean clause has been very controversial: "Whoever repudiates his wife, not by illegitimate unions (πορνεία), and marries another, commits adultery" (*Mt* 19:9; cf. 5:32). After innumerable discussions, no consensus has been reached either on the *porneia* or on the precise consequences it would have. The Latin Tradition has always excluded the possibility of a second union for this reason,[156] subsequent to a valid first union (cf. *Mk* 10:10-11), which is consistent with the perplexity of the disciples according to the text of Matthew (*Mt* 19:10).

137. [*Marriage and the "Mysterion"*]. The very presence of Jesus at the wedding at Cana (*Jn* 2:1-12), with all its meaning of messianic weddings, together with other allusions of a nuptial nature (*Mt* 9:15 and similarly; *Mt* 25:5-6), highlight the capacity of the conjugal relationship to express profound aspects of the mystery of God, such as, for example, his fidelity to our infidelity to his covenant (cf. *Ez* 16 and 23; *Hos* 2; *Jer* 3:1-10; *Is* 54). The

---

[155] International Theological Commission, *Communion and Stewardship: Human Persons Created in the Image of God* [2004], §§ 32-33, 39.

[156] Council of Trent, Session 24. *Doctrine on the Sacrament of Marriage*, canon 7 (DH 1807).

letter to the Ephesians (5:31-32) correlates the marriage covenant expressly with the "mysterion" (*sacramentum*) of the irrevocable covenant between Christ and the Church. From the biblical witness as a whole, the Church has considered indissolubility as a fundamental element of both natural and Christian marriage. The union between man and woman, indissoluble by nature, realises its truth in the fidelity and good of the offspring. After the reception of baptism (of the configuration of the spouses to Christ and their sanctification by the indwelling of the Spirit), it in a certain way becomes by itself a sacramental representation of Christ's fidelity. [157] The love between spouses is no stranger to the new source of their Christian life and faith. In the Christian life, faith and love cannot be dissociated in an absolute way.

138. [*Marriage: qualified by Faith*]. Following St Paul, the Church has also understood the conjugal relationship as something highly qualified by the presence of faith (cf. *1 Cor* 7:12-16). In the case of the marriage of a Christian to a non-Christian, Paul says the following: "An unbelieving husband is sanctified by his wife, and an unbelieving wife is sanctified by a believing husband" (*1 Cor* 7:14). In this passage (esp. *1 Cor* 7:15), the so-called Pauline privilege is based, in which a higher qualification is discerned, in the order of grace, of sacramental marriage over natural marriage.

b) Lights from the Tradition

139. The typical "marrying in the Lord," characteristic of Christians, has been expressed in different ways throughout history. According to the letter to Diognetus, at the beginning Christians did not differentiate: "They marry like everyone else."[158] However, it soon evolved. Already Ignatius of Antioch maintains the convenience of communicating the link to the

---

[157] Cf. Augustine, *De nuptiis et concupiscentia*, I, X, 11 (CSEL 42, 222-224; PL 40, 420).

[158] *Ep. Ad Diognetum*, 5, 6 (Funk, 137).

bishop.[159] Tertullian, for his part, praises the unions that the Church blesses.[160] Beyond the precise interpretation of the scope of the expressions of these early theologians, it is emphasised that the event of marriage was not alien to either the faith of the bride and groom or to the ecclesial community. From the fourth and fifth centuries onwards, the ecclesial blessing, in the figure of a minister, was an established custom.[161] From this period onwards, a Christian liturgy of its own is taking shape,[162] which integrates typically pagan customs and transforms them, as in the case of the "velatio,"[163] the coronation,[164] the handover of the bride, the union of the hands,[165] the blessing of the rings, the arras (wedding coins), or the kiss of the betrothed; at the same time, it adds others, as the presentation to the spouses of the "common cup," which is typical of the Byzantine liturgy.[166] The marriage liturgy, in its prayers and the interpretation of gestures, expresses the singular place of marriage in the divine economy, with allusions to the biblical texts on marriage. Both Peter Lombard and the Second Lateran Council consider marriage as a sacrament; something that both the Council of Florence and

---

[159] *Ep. ad Polycarpum*, 5, 2 (Funk, 107; FuP 1, 186).

[160] *Ad uxorem* II, 8 (CCSL 1, 393; SCh 273, 148).

[161] Cf. Gregory Nazianzus , *Ep.* 231 (PG 37, 373); Ambrosiaster, *Comm. in Epist. I ad Cor.* 7, 40 (PL 17, 225); Id., *Comm. in Epist. I ad Tim.* 3, 12 (PL 17, 470); Pseudo-Augustine, *Quaest. Novi et Veteris Testamenti*, CXXVII (CSEL 50, 400); Ambrose, *Epist. 19 ad Vigilium trident.*, 7 (PL 16, 984-985); Predestinatus, III, 31 (PL 53, 670).

[162] Cf. Sacramentario Reginensis, 316 (*Rerum ecclesiasticarum documenta, series major*, Fontes 4, ed. L.K. Mohlberg, 1447, 1449, 1453); *Hanc igitur* of the Verona Sacramentary, 85 (Mohlberg, 1107).

[163] Cf. *Hadrianeum Sacramentary*, 836 (ed. J Deshusses); Paulinus of Nola, *Carmen* 25, 199-232 (CSEL 30, 244-245).

[164] Cf. John Chrysostom, *In 1 Tim.* Cap. II, hom. IX, 2 (PG 62, 546).

[165] Gregory Nazianzus, *Ep.* 193 (PG 37, 316-318).

[166] For more details, cf. A Raès, *Le marriage, sa célébration et sa spiritualité dans les Églises d'Orient*, Chevetogne 1959 ; K Ritzer, *Formen, Riten und Religiöses Brauchtum der Eheschliessung in den Christlichen Kirchen des ersten Jahrtausends*, Münster 1962; B. Kleinheyer; E. von Severus; R. Kaczynski (eds.), *Gottesdienst der Kirche. Handbuch der Liturgiewissenschaft* 8. *Sakramentliche Feiern* II, Regensburg 1984.

the Council of Trent will endorse with strong conviction.[167] In this last Council, the necessity of the canonical form for the validity of the sacrament is determined, without modifying the doctrinal understanding of the sacrament, thus showing how it is about an ecclesial reality belonging to the order of faith that happens "in facie Ecclesiae,"[168] as opposed to the doctrine of the reformers that considers marriage as a merely civil matter.[169] In this way, the ecclesial character of marriage is recognised, far from understanding it as a private matter between the spouses.

c) Marriage as a Sacrament

140. If the sacraments presuppose faith (SC 59), marriage is no exception: "The shepherds, moved by love for Christ, are to strive to receive the bride and groom and first of all foster and strengthen their faith: for the sacrament of marriage presupposes it and demands it."[170] A marital union between a man and a woman, both non-baptised, from the point of view of the Christian faith, is a tremendously valuable creatural reality, capable of being elevated to the supernatural order, for example, in the case of a later conversion of the spouses. In other words, in "natural" marriage there is a significant reality open to its full realisation and completion in Christ. In the first communities, the reality of marriage is not lived on the margins of faith. Christians live the conjugal covenant "in the Lord" (*1 Cor* 7:39). Certain public behaviours that are contrary to the faith in the context of couple relationships can lead to excommunication from the community

---

[167] Peter Lombard, *Summa Sententiarum* IV. d. 2 and 26 (PL 192, 842 AND 908); Lateran II, canon 23 (DH 718); Council of Florence, *Decrees for the Armenians* (DH 1327); Council of Trent, session 7. *Decrees on the Sacraments. Canons on the Sacraments in general*, canon 1 (DH 1601).

[168] Council of Trent, Session 24 *Canons on Reformation of Marriage. Decree "Tametsi"* (DH 1813-1816).

[169] Martin Luther, *De captivitate babylonica, De matrimonio* (WA 6,550); John Calvin, *Inst. Christ. Lib.* IV, c. 19, 34 (Corp. Reform. 32, 1121).

[170] *Ordo celebrandi matrimonium, Praenotanda* § 16 (Typis Polyglottis Vaticanis, 1989), with reference to Vatican II, Const. *Sacrosantum concilium*, 59. The very idea of the *Praenotanda* § 7 of 1969.

(*1 Cor* 5). For conjugal love between Christian spouses has become a sign, a sacrament, which expresses Christ's love for his Church. This sign of an irrevocable love only expresses what it means if this same bond is indissoluble. Indissolubility is an aspect already present "from the beginning" in the divine plan and which, therefore, essentially configures the reality of every authentic marriage in its theological nucleus. In this way, that human reality as deep as the love of a couple, so characteristic of our relational being, the capacity for mutual self-giving between spouses and children, expresses the deepest part of the divine mystery: love.

141. Two baptised Catholics confirmed and with a habitual Eucharistic praxis, take a beautiful and significant step forward in their life of faith when they celebrate their marriage. They receive the grace of the sacrament of marriage, which consists basically in that they now "manifest and share in the mystery of the unity of the fruitful love between Christ and the Church (*Eph* 5:32), they help each other to sanctify themselves in conjugal life and in the procreation of children."[171] Their paths of faith have come together to witness to the power of Christ's love for the Church, for mutual enrichment, for Christian education of children and for mutual sanctification.[172] They form a "domestic Church";[173] "They are fortified and consecrated by a special sacrament" (GS 48). In this way they give concrete expression to the maturity of the faith proper to Confirmation, assuming a state of Christian life (cf. LG 11) and some responsibilities in the Christian community. In the celebration of their marriage, their faith is presupposed, expressed, nourished and strengthened by the action of Christ in the sacrament, who "abides with them"(GS 48), with the marriage covenant and with family

---

[171] Vatican II, Dogmatic Constitution *Lumen gentium*, 11; cf. Ibid, 41; *Catechism of the Catholic Church*, 1641-1642.

[172] Cf. Pius XI, Encyclical *Casti connubii* (31st December 1930): AAS 22 (1930), 583.

[173] Cf. *Acts* 16:15; 18:8; Vatican II, Dogmatic Constitution *Lumen gentium*, 11; *Catechism of the Catholic Church*, 1655-1657.

life that they now undertake under the blessing of God and the Church. Catholic marriage expresses with intensity that it is a project of life conceived and encouraged from the faith,[174] as a way of mutual sanctification, in which the spouses exercise the common priesthood by giving each other the sacrament[175] (cf. LG 10). The consciousness and purpose of being a sacrament of God's love presuppose and express the personal faith of each of the spouses. Thus, it truly appears as a sacrament of faith, in which Jesus Christ and the Holy Spirit, the Spirit of Love (cf. *Rom* 5:5), act effectively. The love that the spouses profess for each other is already determined by their reality as baptised. The sanctification brought about by the sacrament impels this supernatural love in the realisation of the conjugal and family community.

d) Faith and the Goods of Marriage

142. The presence of faith and the efficacious action of sacramental grace impel the spouses to realise the goods proper to marriage: "As a mutual gift of two persons, this intimate union and the good of the children impose total fidelity on the spouses and argue for an unbreakable oneness between them" (GS 48). Indissolubility (cf. GS 49) is understood from the point of view of faith as the essential note of conjugal relationship, because otherwise it would deviate from God's original plan (*Gn* 2:23-24) and would cease to be a visible sign of Christ's irrevocable love for his Church. Fidelity between spouses and the generous search for the good of the other spouse (cf. GS 49) is lived as something that flows gently and congruently from faith and personal relationship with the Lord Jesus. For faith puts us in a personal relationship with Jesus Christ, while presenting as a model of following the One who gave his life for sinners (e.g., *Mk* 10:45; *Rom* 5:6-8; 14:15; *Eph* 5:2; 1 *Jn* 4:9-10). Christian husbands and wives from faith try to translate into their married

---

[174] Cf. Francis, Apostolic Exhortation *Amoris laetitia* (19th March 2016) 218: AAS 108 (2016), 398-399.

[175] Cf. Francis, Apostolic Exhortation *Gaudete et exsultate* (19th March 2018) 141.

and family life the maxim according to which "there is more joy in giving than in receiving" (*Acts* 20:35). By faith we know fertility is inscribed in God's plan (*Gn* 1:28), one of whose signs of blessing is offspring. The love of the Trinitarian God teaches us, through faith, that true love always includes the maximum loving reciprocity and the maximum openness towards the other. For this reason, faith prevents us from understanding marriage as a kind of calculated couple selfishness. An active faith of both spouses includes an understanding that God, as the author of marriage, "has endowed it with various goods and ends" (GS 48) which Christian spouses strive to live and unfold. As a result, a living and shared faith in the realm of marital union reduces the possibility that egocentric or individualistic tendencies will take root in each spouse as well as in the couple, even in spite of the environmental pressure of the surrounding culture.

4.2. A QUAESTIO DUBIA: THE SACRAMENTAL QUALITY OF THE MARRIAGE OF THE "BAPTISED NON-BELIEVERS"

a) Approach to the Question

143. [*Definition*]. Marriage is a creatural reality. By baptism the natural bond is elevated to a supernatural sign: "The matrimonial covenant, by which a man and a woman establish between themselves a partnership of the whole of life, is by its nature ordered toward the good of the spouses and the procreation and education of offspring; this covenant between baptised persons has been raised by Christ the Lord to the dignity of a sacrament."[176] According to the theological doctrine and canonical practise currently in force, every valid marriage contract between baptised persons is "by itself" sacrament,[177] even in the absence of faith of the contracting parties. That is to say, in the

---

[176] *Catechism of the Catholic Church*, 1601; cites literally the Code of Canon Law, canon 1055, § 1.

[177] "Quare inter baptizatos nequit matrimonialis contractus validus consistere, quin sit eo ipso sacramentum" (CIC, canon 1055, § 2).

case of the baptised the inseparability between a valid marriage contract, corresponding to the creatural order of marriage, and the sacrament is affirmed. The baptised could not simultaneously have entered into the sacramental order, by baptism, without this affecting such a reality that is so determinative of life and capable of sacramental significance, such as marriage, which would be removed from the sacramental order to which the spouses irrevocably belong after baptism (cf. §§166 d and 167 d). Should this doctrine also be applied to the case of the marriage union between "baptised non-believers"? In this delicate matter, the "reciprocity between faith and sacraments" that we have been defending seems to be called into question. In order to approach the question in an appropriate way, we need to clarify the status and terms of the question in a more detailed way.

144. [*"Baptised non-believers"*]. By "baptised non-believers" we mean those persons in whom there is no sign of the presence of the dialogical nature of faith, proper to the personal response of the believer to the sacramental interlocution of the Trinitarian God, as we explained in the second chapter. This category includes two types of people. Those who received baptism in infancy, but subsequently, for whatever reason, have not come to perform a personal act of faith, involving their understanding and their will. This is a very frequent case in traditionally Christian countries, where a very broad de-Christianisation of society is accompanied by a great negligence in education in the faith. We also refer to those baptised persons who consciously deny the faith explicitly and do not consider themselves to be Catholic or Christian believers. They even sometimes perform a formal act of abandonment of the Catholic faith and separation from the Church, without the reason for the act of formal abandonment of the Catholic Church being entry into another church, community, or Christian denomination. In both cases the presence of a "disposition to believe"[178] is not perceived.

---

[178] Cf. International Theological Commission, *Doctrine on Christian Marriage* [1977], § 2.3.

145. [*Preliminary Formulation of the Question*]. Thus, the question that arises is if two unmarried "baptised non-believers" of different sexes of either of the two types described are married by a sacramental celebration or by some other valid form of union: does a sacrament take place? The topic is the subject of debate and has generated an abundant literature. Its solution is not clear, since several major elements come into play in simultaneous interaction. Next, we will go through some significant milestones of its development in recent years, in the teachings of the last pontiffs, as well as in official ecclesial instances, in order to take responsibility with the terms of the question.

b) The State and terms of the Question

146. [*International Theological Commission*]. In 1977, the International Theological Commission produced a document entitled *Propositions on the Doctrine of Christian Marriage.* Among the topics discussed are: the sacramentality of marriage, marriage between "baptised non-believers," and the inseparability between contract and sacrament. They supported a series of highly nuanced theses that hint at the tension between the conviction of the necessity of faith for the celebration of a sacrament and the reluctance to declare faith as the determinant of the sacramentality of marriage. From their affirmations, which we do not reproduce in their entirety, the following stand out for our topic.

147. The existence of a constitutive and reciprocal relationship between indissolubility and sacramentality. And they specified: "sacramentality constitutes the final grounds, although not the only grounds, for its indissolubility" (§ 2.2.).

148. Regarding the interrelationship between faith and the sacrament of marriage, they held that in the sacrament of marriage the source of grace is Jesus Christ, not the faith of the contracting subjects. And they added: "That, however, does not mean that grace is conferred in the sacrament of matrimony

103

outside of faith or in the absence of faith" (§ 2.3.). Faith would be a "dispositive cause" for fruitfulness not for validity.

149. About the "baptised non believers," they said:

The existence today of "baptised non-believers" raises a new theological problem and a grave pastoral dilemma, especially when the lack of, or rather the rejection of, the Faith seems clear. The intention of carrying out what Christ and the Church desires is the minimum condition required before consent is considered to be a "real human act" on the sacramental plane. The problem of intention and that of the personal faith of the contracting parties must not be confused, but they must not be totally separated. *In the last analysis the real intention is born from and feeds on living faith.* Where there is no trace of faith (in the sense of "belief" – being disposed to believe), and no desire for grace or salvation is found, then a real doubt arises as to whether there is the above-mentioned general and truly sacramental intention and whether the contracted marriage is validly contracted or not. As was noted, the personal faith of the contracting parties does not constitute the sacramentality of matrimony, but the absence of personal faith compromises the validity of the sacrament (§2.3. Emphasis added).

In his commentary, published along with the document, the then secretary of the Commission, Msgr. Philippe Delhaye, states: "The key to the problem is in the intention; the intention to do what the Church does by offering a permanent sacrament that entails indissolubility, fidelity, fruitfulness."[179]

150. Later, the Commission document reaffirms the inseparability between contract and sacrament: "For the Church, no natural marriage separated from the sacrament exists for baptised persons, but only natural marriage elevated to the dignity of a sacrament"(§ 3.5.).

---

[179] *Comentario* II (in the Spanish edition: Comisión Teológica Internacional, Documentos 1969-1996, ed. C. Pozo, Madrid 1998, 195).

151. [*St John Paul II*]. Throughout the pontificate of John Paul II, the subject of marriage of the "baptised non-believers" and the need for faith for the sacrament of matrimony came up repeatedly. Proposition 12.4 approved by the Fifth Ordinary General Assembly of the Synod of Bishops, held in 1980, which dealt with the family said: "Let there be examined more seriously if the assertion that a valid marriage between baptised persons is always a sacrament also applies to those who have lost faith. Let the juridical and pastoral consequences be drawn from it."[180]

152. In the post-synodal exhortation, *Familiaris consortio*, John Paul II will argue consistently that the marriage act is intrinsically qualified by the supernatural reality to which the baptised belong irrevocably, beyond the express awareness of this reality.[181] On our subject, it clearly indicates:

As for wishing to lay down further criteria for admission to the ecclesial celebration of marriage, criteria that would concern the level of faith of those to be married, this would above all involve grave risks. In the first place, the risk of making unfounded and discriminatory judgements; secondly, the risk of causing doubts about the validity of marriages already celebrated, with grave harm to Christian communities, and new and unjustified anxieties to the consciences of married couples; one would also fall into the danger of calling into question the sacramental nature of many marriages of brethren separated from full communion with the Catholic Church, thus contradicting ecclesial tradition.[182]

---

[180] "Las 43 proposiciones del Sínodo de los obispos sobre la familia": *Ecclesia*, no. 2039 (18th and 25th July 1981) 894. Proposition 12.4 was adopted with 196 votes in favour, 7 against and 3 abstentions. ("Les 43 propositions du Synode des évêques sur la famille": *La Documentation Catholique* 1809 [7th June 1981] 540). See proposition 12 in its entirety, which deals directly with our topic.

[181] St John Paul II, Apostolic Exhortation *Familiaris consortio* (22nd November 1981) 13 and 68: AAS 74 (1982), 93-96 and 163-165.

[182] St John Paul II, Apostolic Exhortation *Familiaris consortio* (22nd November 1981) 68: AAS 74 (1982), 164-165.

153. In spite of everything, he does not fail to recognise the possibility that the bride and groom simultaneously ask for the ecclesial celebration of marriage and "show that they reject explicitly and formally what the Church intends to do when the marriage of baptised persons is celebrated." In this case he prescribes: "the pastor of souls cannot admit them to the celebration of marriage."[183] We can interpret that because in that case there would be no true sacrament. That is to say, John Paul II demands some minimums, even if it is only the absence of explicit and formal rejection of what the Church does. In his own way, therefore, he also rejects what we can call an absolute sacramental automatism.[184]

154. Later, in an important address to the Roman Rota (30th January 2003), he clearly warned of the non-existence of two types of marriages, one natural and the other supernatural: "The church does not refuse to celebrate a marriage for the person who is *well disposed*, even if he is imperfectly prepared from the supernatural point of view, provided the person has the *right intention to marry according to the natural reality of marriage*. In fact, alongside natural marriage, one cannot describe another model of Christian marriage with specific supernatural requisites."[185] This opinion had already been clearly defended by John Paul II in another address to the Roman Rota (1st February 2001).[186] In 2001, he stressed that faith should not be demanded as a minimum requirement, because it is something alien to tradition.[187] He ratified the natural purpose

---

[183] Ibid., 165.

[184] Cf. Council of Trent, Session 7. *Canons on the Sacraments in general,* canon 6 (DH 1606). See note 82.

[185] St John Paul II, *Address to the Prelate Auditors, Officials and Advocates of the Tribunal of the Roman Rota,* 30th January 2003, § 8: AAS 95 (2003), 397. The first italics are in the original. The last ones are ours.

[186] St John Paul II, *Address of John Paul II to the Prelate Auditors, Officials and Advocates of the Tribunal of the Roman Rota,* 1st February 2001: AAS 93 (2001), 358-364.

[187] St John Paul II, *Address of John Paul II to the Prelate Auditors, Officials and Advocates of the Tribunal of the Roman Rota,* 1st February 2001, § 8: AAS 93 (2001), 363.

of marriage and that marriage consists of a natural reality, not exclusively supernatural. In this context he said: "To obscure the natural dimension of marriage, therefore, with its reduction to a mere subjective experience, also entails the implicit denial of its sacramentality."[188] That is to say, the basis of everything lies in the natural, creational reality.

155. *[The creation of the Code of Canon Law]*. In the work leading up to the drafting of the Code of Canon Law, the question of the inseparability between the natural reality of marriage and sacramental marriage as a salvific reality was discussed extensively. In the end, the legislator chose to maintain the most common doctrine, without attempting to elucidate the issue doctrinally, as it was not within his competence. When legislating, the most commonly accepted theological presuppositions are included.[189] This inseparability was discussed during the Council of Trent. Among its opponents, the figure of Melchior Cano stands out. It has not been defined, although it is the most constant opinion. Many qualify it as Catholic doctrine.[190] The Code of Canon Law picks it up in canon 1055, § 2, already mentioned.[191]

156. *[The jurisprudence of the Roman Rota]*. The jurisprudence of the Rota, following Catholic doctrine, considers indissolubility to be an essential property of natural marriage. However, in a highly secularised social and cultural context, in which convictions very different from those of the Church are widespread and ingrained, the question arises whether *de facto*, in the absence of faith, the indissolubility of marriage is accepted. Thus, for some years now, jurisprudence has held that lack of faith may affect the intention to enter into a natural marriage.[192] In a way,

---

[188] St John Paul II, *Address of John Paul II to the Prelate Auditors, Officials and Advocates of the Tribunal of the Roman Rota*, 1st February 2001, § 8: AAS 93 (2001), 364.

[189] Cf. *Communicationes*, 9 (1977), 122.

[190] Cf. *Communicationes*, 15 (1983), 222.

[191] See note 177.

[192] Sentence *coram* Stankiewicz, 19th April 1991: SRRD 83, 280-290.

it seems to echo the sensitivity expressed in proposition 40 of the XI General Assembly of the Synod of Bishops, which took place in October 2005, under the pontificate of Benedict XVI, and dealt with the Eucharist. In it, in response to the issue of the divorced and remarried, it was said:

> The Synod hopes that all possible efforts will be made to ensure the pastoral character, presence and correct and solicitous activity of the ecclesiastical tribunals in regard to causes of marital annulment (cf. "Dignitas connubi"), both by further deepening the essential elements for the validity of marriage, and also by taking into account *the problems arising from the context of profound anthropological transformation of our time, by which the faithful themselves run the risk of being conditioned, especially if they lack a solid Christian formation.*[193]

157. [*Joseph Ratzinger-Benedict XVI*]. The then Prefect of the Congregation for the Doctrine of the Faith, Cardinal Joseph Ratzinger, stated clearly in 1997: "It needs to be clarified whether every marriage between two baptised persons is '*ipso facto*' a sacramental marriage. In fact, the Code states that only the 'valid' marriage between baptised persons is at the same time a Sacrament (cf. CIC, canon 1055 § 2). Faith belongs to the essence of the sacrament; what remains to be clarified is the juridical question of what evidence of 'absence of faith' would have as a consequence that the sacrament does not come into being."[194] An opinion that he qualified as Pope, Benedict XVI, in an address to priests in 2005, indicating that the problem is very difficult; and that he now had more doubts about faith as a reason for invalidity and that the question still requires deepening.[195]

---

[193] "Proposiciones del Sínodo de los Obispos sobre la Eucaristía": *Ecclesia* no. 3284 (19th November 2005), 34. Emphasis added.

[194] Joseph Ratzinger, "Introduction," In Congregation for the Doctrine of the Faith, *Sobre la atención pastoral de los divorciados vueltos a casar*. Documentos, comentarios y estudios, Madrid 2000, 34.

[195] Benedict XVI, *Address to Diocesan Clergy of Aosta*, 25th July 2005: AAS 97 (2005), 856.

158. In his last address to the Roman Rota,[196] Pope Benedict XVI once again elaborated on this issue, which was so important to him. We extracted some of his contributions. At the beginning of his reflections, he alludes to the question of faith and intention, in line with the International Theological Commission, whose document he mentions:

The indissoluble pact between a man and a woman does not, for the purposes of the sacrament, require of those engaged to be married, their personal faith; what it does require, as a necessary minimal condition, is the intention to do what the Church does. However, whilst it is important not to confuse the problem of the intention with that of the personal faith of those contracting marriage, it is nonetheless impossible to separate them completely.[197]

159. He then explains how faith and openness to God greatly determine the conception of life in all its facets and specifically in something as delicate as a lifelong bond (indissolubility, exclusivity, and fidelity). "The rejection of the divine proposal, in fact, leads to a profound imbalance in all human relations, including matrimonial relations, and facilitates an erroneous understanding of liberty and of self-fulfilment." From there it follows, according to Benedict XVI, "a profound imbalance in all human relations, including matrimonial relations." And "it facilitates an erroneous understanding of liberty and of self-fulfilment which, together with flight from the patient tolerance of suffering, condemns people to withdraw into selfish egocentricity."[198]

---

[196] Benedict XVI, *Address to the Tribunal of the Roman Rota*, 26th January 2013: AAS 105 (2013), 168-172.

[197] Benedict XVI, *Address to the Tribunal of the Roman Rota*, 26th January 2013, § 1: AAS 105 (2013), 168.

[198] Benedict XVI, *Address to the Tribunal of the Roman Rota*, 26th January 2013, § 2: AAS 105 (2013), 169-170.

160. This lack of faith does not automatically lead to the impossibility of a natural marriage. However:

> Faith in God, sustained by divine grace, is thus a very important element for living mutual dedication and conjugal fidelity. (...) Yet, closure to God or the rejection of the sacred dimension of the conjugal union and of its value in the order of grace certainly makes arduous the practical embodiment of the most lofty model of marriage conceived by the Church according to God's plan and can even undermine the actual validity of the pact, should it be expressed, as the consolidated jurisprudence of this Tribunal assumes, in a rejection of the principle of the conjugal obligation of fidelity itself, that is, of the other essential elements or properties of matrimony.[199]

161. Later on, he explores how faith decisively affects the good of the spouses: "In truth, there is in the resolve of Christian spouses to live a real *communio coniugalis* a dynamism proper to faith, for which the *confessio*, the sincere personal response to the announcement of salvation, involves the believer in the impetus of God's love."[200] He goes on to affirm how confession of faith, far from remaining on an abstract level, fully involves the person in confessed charity, since truth and love are inseparable. And he concludes: "One must not, therefore, disregard the consideration that can arise in the cases in which, precisely because of the absence of faith, the good of the spouses is jeopardised, that is, excluded from the consent itself."[201] In such a way that the lack of faith "may, although not necessarily, also damage the goods of marriage, since the reference to the natural order desired by God is inherent in the conjugal pact (cf. *Gn* 2:24)."[202]

---

[199] Benedict XVI, *Address to the Tribunal of the Roman Rota*, 26th January 2013, § 2: AAS 105 (2013), 170.

[200] Benedict XVI, *Address to the Tribunal of the Roman Rota*, 26th January 2013, § 3: AAS 105 (2013), 171.

[201] Benedict XVI, *Address to the Tribunal of the Roman Rota*, 26th January 2013, § 4: AAS 105 (2013), 172.

[202] Ibid.

162. [*Pope Francis*]. The need for further study, requested by Benedict XVI, is still valid, according to the findings prior to the last synodal assemblies on the family and the statements of Pope Francis. Thus, the *Intrumentum laboris* for the III Extraordinary General Assembly of the Synod of Bishops (2014) summarised our question: "Very many responses, especially in Europe and North America…they see a need to investigate the question of the relationship between faith and the Sacrament of Matrimony, as suggested by Pope Benedict XVI."[203] The *Relatio Synodi*, which serves both as the conclusion of the III Extraordinary General Assembly and as the *Lineamenta* for the XIV General Assembly of the Synod, also alludes to the question[204]; so does the *Intrumentum laboris* for the XIV Assembly (2015).[205] The post-synodal exhortation *Amoris laetitia* warns in its introduction: "The complexity of the issues that arose [during the synodal path] revealed the need for continued open discussion of a number of doctrinal, moral, spiritual, and pastoral questions."[206] And it adds: "This having been said, there is a need for further reflection on God's action in the marriage rite; this is clearly manifested in the Oriental Churches through the importance of the blessing that the couple receive as a sign of the gift of the Spirit."[207] The present reflection on "reciprocity between faith and marriage" is modestly situated on this path.

---

[203] III Extraordinary General Assembly of the Synod of Bishops on *The Pastoral Challenges of the Family in the Context of Evangelisation*. *Instrumentum laboris* (2014), 96 (*Ecclesia* no. 3735-3736 [12th and 19th July 2014], 1065-1066).

[204] "Among other proposals, the role which faith plays in persons who marry could possibly be examined in ascertaining the validity of the Sacrament of Marriage, all the while maintaining that the marriage of two baptised Christians is always a sacrament" (*Relatio Synodi*, 48:AAS 106 (2014), 904).

[205] XIV Ordinary General Assembly of the Synod of Bishops on *The Vocation and Mission of the Family in the Church and the Contemporary World. Instrumentum laboris* (2015), 114-115 (Ecclesia no. 3795-3796 [5th and 12th September 2015] 1356).

[206] Francis, Apostolic Exhortation *Amoris laetitia* (19th March 2016) 2: AAS 108 (2016), 311.

[207] Francis, Apostolic Exhortation *Amoris laetitia* (19th March 2016) 75: AAS 108 (2016), 341.

163. Pope Francis has also addressed our issue in various circumstances. In his address to the Roman Rota on 23rd January 2015,[208] he referred to the possible defects of origin in consent, which can affect validity, pointing out how it can be given "both directly as a defect of valid intention, as well as by grave deficit in the understanding of marriage itself to such an extent that this is what dictates one's will (cf. canon 1099)."[209] And he added: "Indeed, at the root of the crisis of marriage is often a *crisis of knowledge enlightened by faith*, that is, knowledge informed by the adhesion to God and his design of love realised in Jesus Christ."[210]

164. Following this line, the apostolic letter in the form of a motu proprio *Mitis iudex Dominus Iesus*[211] (15th August 2015), states: "Among the circumstances of things and persons that can allow a case for nullity of marriage to be handled by means of the briefer process according to canons 1683-1687, are included, for example: the defect of faith which can generate simulation of consent or error that determines the will."[212] Thus, lack of faith may be decisive for validity.

165. In the following year (22nd January 2016), when speaking to the Roman Rota,[213] he expressed himself in this sense: "It is worth clearly reiterating that the essential component of marital consent is not the quality of one's faith, which according to unchanging doctrine can be undermined only on the plane of the natural (cf. CIC, canon 1055 § 1 and 2)."[214] And he made

---

[208] Francis, *Address to the Officials of the Tribunal of the Roman Rota*, 23rd January 2015: AAS 107 (2015), 182-185.

[209] Ibid., 182-183.

[210] Ibid., 183. Emphasis added.

[211] Francis, Apostolic Letter motu propio *Mitis iudex Dominus Iesus* (15th August 2015) : AAS 107 (2015), 958-970.

[212] Art. 14, § 1: AAS 107 (2015) 969.

[213] Francis, *Address to the Officials of the Tribunal of the Roman Rota*, 22nd January 2016: AAS 108 (2016) 136-139.

[214] Ibid., 138-139.

his own the doctrine that holds the presence of the *habitus fidei* operative after baptism, even without a psychologically perceptible faith. And he concludes: "A lack of formation in the faith and error with respect to the unity, indissolubility and sacramental dignity of marriage invalidates marital consent only if they influence the person's will (cf. CIC, canon 1099). It is for this reason that errors regarding the sacramentality of marriage must be evaluated very attentively."[215]

166. [*The terms of the question*]. From this brief overview of the teaching of the last pontiffs on our subject, as well as from official ecclesial instances, it seems clear that the fundamental issue is not entirely resolved, although it is quite focused. By making an interpretative and systematising balance, these aspects come into play in dynamic interrelation and dynamic tension:

a) As in every sacrament, in marriage there is a transmission of the grace of Christ. This grace is not due to the faith of the ministers, according to the Latin tradition of the contracting parties, but is a gift of Christ, who is actively present in the conjugal covenant, and of the Spirit.

b) There can be no sacrament without faith. A kind of sacramental automatism would deny the dialogical nature of the sacramental economy, which is structured around the intimate connection between faith and sacraments (cf. chapter 2). Thus, in order for there to be a sacrament in the case of marriage between "baptised non-believers," there must be some active faith, regardless of the difficulty in determining it positively, either in the spouses or adjudicating it in its totality to Mother Church.

c) The practical difficulty of verifying the lack of faith of the spouses is a difficult and complex pastoral problem (cf. § 61). However, it is up to theology dogmatically to clarify

---

[215] Ibid., 139.

this very nuclear point for a proper understanding of the sacrament of marriage.

d) Validly received baptism has irrevocably grafted the baptised into the sacramental economy with the impression of "character" (cf. § 65). His personal reality, beyond his conscious acts of understanding and will, proper to faith,[216] is already marked by this belonging without sin or the absence of faith, whether shapeless or formed, being able to erase or annul what the irrevocable gift of Christ has produced.

e) The most established Catholic doctrine maintains the inseparability between contract and sacrament (cf. § 155). The definitive clarification of this aspect is still pending. The separation between contract and sacrament would have a direct impact on the question we are dealing with. Given the present state of Catholic doctrine, it seems appropriate to adhere to the most common opinion today regarding the inseparability between contract and sacrament.

f) The faith of the spouses is decisive for the fruitfulness of the sacrament (cf. § 68). Validity and, with it, sacramentality depends on whether a true marriage bond has taken place: a natural marriage.

g) The minimum necessary for a sacrament is the intention to enter into a true natural marriage (cf. § 154).

h) In the case of the sacrament of matrimony, faith and intention cannot be identified, but neither can they be completely separated (cf. §§ 149 and 158). Since it is clear that the sacramental truth of marriage hangs on intention and that faith influences intention, it is not entirely clear how and to what extent lack of faith affects intention.

We propose to deepen on this last point for the case of the described "baptised non-believers" (cf. § 144). This is an

---

[216] Cf. St Thomas Aquinas, *ST* II-II, q.4, a.4.

aspect that is congruent with the reciprocity between faith and sacraments that we have been defending.

167. [*Possible Theoretical Alternatives to Resolve the Issue*]. But first, to complete, let us look at the list of possible theoretical solutions to our topic and its theological solvency, measured from the theological perspective that we have previously based and we are shuffling (chapter 2).

a) First, an absolute sacramental automatism could be defended. The fact of baptism would imply, regardless of the faith of the spouses, that the marriage contract is elevated "*eo ipso*" to the supernatural reality of the sacrament. This solution clashes with the dialogical nature of the sacramental economy, which we have explained reasonably, so we discard it.

b) A second possibility would be to defend the separation between contract and sacrament. Since it is true that the identity between contract and sacrament has not been solemnly defined, in order to consider this separation as theologically certain, it would be necessary to provide a specific convincing argument in this regard. We renounce exploring that avenue and follow the most common terms of current Catholic theology about marriage.

c) A third option would assert the presence of the ecclesial faith, despite the absence of a personal faith of the contracting parties. There would be a substitution of the ecclesial faith, in spite of the lack of a personal faith on the part of the contracting parties. This option, however, also presents its problems. On the one hand, the essence of the sacrament is given in the consent between the spouses. On this basis, the Church can demand certain formal requirements for its validity, as in fact happens today, as the fruit of a long history. On the other hand, throughout the exploration of the dialogical nature of the sacramental economy (chapter 2), we have shown how ecclesial faith precedes and accompanies personal faith, but never supplants it completely. To attribute the sacramentality of marriage exclusively to the ecclesial faith would imply denying the interpersonal nature of the sacramental economy.

d) A fourth possibility lies in attributing sacramentality to the efficacy linked to the "character" impressed with baptism. The "character" is due to the irrevocability of Christ's gift. It implies insertion into the sacramental realty of economy. It empowers the dialogical exercise of sacramentality, without by itself implying an active exercise of the sacramentality. The *habitus*, linked to the "character," is a disposition to act; it is neither a performance nor an act. It requires that it be exercised by a power, such as the will.[217] Thus, with the impression of the "character" and the instilling of habit, the sacramental interlocution on the part of God is affirmed, with all certainty, but the dialogical response of a personal nature on the part of the graced subject is lacking. He has nevertheless remained capable of acting on this response.

e) As we have already anticipated, there remains the possibility of arguing about the intention, since for the validity of every sacrament there has to be the intention of doing what the Church intends in each sacrament.

4.3. THE INTENTION AND THE ESTABLISHMENT OF THE MATRIMONIAL BOND IN THE ABSENCE OF FAITH

a) The Intention is necessary for there to be a Sacrament

168. [*Necessity of Intention*]. As we have said[218] (§§ 67-69), the traditional doctrine of the sacraments includes the conviction that the sacrament requires at least the intention to do what the Church does: "All these sacraments are realised by three elements: of things, as matter; of words, as form; and of the

---

[217] Cf. St Thomas Aquinas, *ST* I-II, q.49-51.

[218] Cf. also § 86 and the text quoted from Cyril of Jerusalem, referring to baptism.

person of the minister who confers the sacrament with the intention of doing what the Church does (*cum intentione faciendi quod facit Ecclesia*). If one of them is missing, the sacrament is not performed."[219] According to the common opinion of Latin theology, the ministers of the sacrament of marriage are the spouses, who reciprocally donate their marriage.[220] In the case of sacramental marriage, at least the intention to perform a natural marriage is required. Now, natural marriage, as the Church understands it, includes as essential properties indissolubility, fidelity and ordering to the good of the spouses, and the good of the offspring. Therefore, if the intention to enter into marriage does not include these properties, at least implicitly, there is a serious lack of intention, capable of calling into question the very existence of natural marriage, which is the necessary basis for sacramental marriage.[221]

169. [*Interrelation between Faith and Intention*]. With varied emphasis, the Magisterium of the last three pontiffs confirms the interconnection between a living and explicit faith and the intention to celebrate a true natural marriage. One that is indissoluble and exclusive and focused on the good of the spouses, through a sincere self-giving charity, and open to offspring. John Paul II asks not to accept spouses who reject "explicitly and formally what the Church intends to do when the marriage of baptised persons is celebrated" (cf. § 153), while maintaining the necessity of having "the right intention to marry according to the natural reality of marriage" (cf. § 154). Benedict XVI notes the remarkable impact of the absence of faith on the conception of life, on relationships, on the very bond of marriage and on the good of the spouses, which can also "damage the goods of marriage" (cf. § 161). Francis points how the root of the marriage crisis lies in the "a crisis of knowledge enlightened by faith" (cf. § 163) and invokes lack of faith as a possible motive

---

[219] Council of Florence, Bull *Exsultate Deo* on Union with the Armenians (DH 1312).
[220] Cf. *Catechism of the Catholic Church*, 1623.
[221] Cf. CIC, canon 1101.

for simulation in consent (cf. § 164). The jurisprudence of the Roman Rota follows the line taken by Benedict XVI (cf. § 156). To be more precise, the aforementioned ecclesial instances and the last two pontiffs consider that the lack of living and explicit faith raises well-founded suspicions about the intention of truly celebrating an indissoluble, definitive and exclusive marriage, as a free reciprocal gift and open to offspring, even though at the root they do not rule out the possibility of this happening. In no case does a simplistic sacramental automatism arise.

b) Predominant Cultural Understanding of Marriage

170. [Predominant Culture and Understanding of Marriage]. In countries whose predominant culture proposes polygamy as a value, which is opposed to the divine plan (cf. Gn 1:26; 2:18-24), it seems more difficult to consider that in the absence of explicit faith, the intention to enter into marriage includes in itself the exclusivity inherent in natural marriage according to the Christian conception. Furthermore, the cultural context of polygamy, together with other aspects that can occur independently of polygamy, clashes with the "principle of parity" of the spouses, rooted in the fact of creation in the image and likeness of God.[222] This is inherent in the very good of the spouses (bonum coniugum), and is one of the fundamental goods of natural marriage. On the other hand, a kind of practical exercise of polygamy, as a factual reality, has spread to many western countries, where the existence of a marriage or couple bond is not understood as an obstacle to living simultaneously other realities, which, according to the Church, belong exclusively to the conjugal order.

171. Years ago, in traditionally Christian countries there was a consensus on the reality of marriage, which was informed by the influence exerted by the Christian faith in society. In

---

[222] Cf. International Theological Commission, Communion and Stewardship: Human Persons Created in the Image of God [2004], §§ 32-39.

this context, it could be assumed that every natural marriage, irrespective of a living and explicit life of faith, included in its intention the properties of natural marriage as understood by the Church. Today, with the entrenchment and diffusion of other conceptions about the family clearly divergent from the Catholic one, greater caution is imposed, generating new doctrinal and pastoral problems.

172. The fact that marriage is a creative reality implies that anthropology is an intrinsic part of its essence in a double sense, closely linked to each other. On the one hand, the conception of the human person comes fully into play, someone who, as a relational being, fulfils his or her own being in self-giving. On the other hand, the essence of marriage is also touched by the understanding of sexual differentiation, male and female, as an element of the divine plan oriented towards procreation and towards the conjugal covenant, as a reflection of God's covenant with the people of Israel and of Christ's covenant with the Church. Both elements come fully into play in natural marriage. It is indissoluble, exclusive, focused on the reciprocal good of the spouses, through interpersonal love, and on the offspring. Thus, the Church appears, sometime alone and under attack, as the cultural bulwark that preserves the natural reality proper to marriage. However, without falling into catastrophic lamentations, a sincere look at our cultural context cannot fail to see how there are increasingly consolidated as unquestionable axioms in postmodern culture, aspects that lead to questioning the natural basis of marriage in its anthropological root. Thus, without the intention of exhaustiveness, the predominant tendency includes as evident, for example, these widespread convictions, rooted and sometimes sanctioned by legislation, clearly contrary to the Catholic faith.

a) The search for personal self-realisation, centred on the satisfaction of the self, as the major goal of life, which justifies the most substantive ethical decisions, also in the field of marriage and family. This conception is opposed to the meaning of loving sacrifice and oblation as the greatest achievement of the truth of the person, which the Christian faith proposes, thus achieving in a magnificent way its meaning and fulfilment.

b) A "macho" type mentality that undervalues women, damaging conjugal parity linked to the good of the spouses, understanding marriage as an alliance between two who would not be equal by divine design, nature and juridical rights, versus the biblical conception and Christian faith.[223] Jesus's counter-cultural stance against divorce (cf. *Mt* 19:3-8) was a defence of the weakest part of the culture of the time: the woman.

c) A "gender ideology" that denies any biological determination of sexual character in the construction of gender identity, undermining the complementarity between the sexes inscribed in the Creator's plan.

d) A divorce mentality, which undermines the understanding of marital indissolubility. On the contrary, it leads to consider the conjugal ties, more commonly known as "living together," as essentially revisable realities, in direct contradiction with the teaching of Jesus in this regard in *Mk* 10:9 and *Mt* 19:6 (cf. *Gn* 2:24).

e) A conception of the body as absolute personal property, freely available to obtain maximum pleasure, especially in the field of sexual relations, detached from an institutional and stable conjugal bond. Paul, however, affirms the belonging of the body to the Lord, excluding immorality (πορνεία), in such a way that the body becomes a channel for the glorification of God (cf. *1 Cor* 6:13-20).

---

[223] Cf. Benedict XVI, *Address to the Tribunal of the Roman Rota* (26th January 2013) § 3: AAS 105 (2013), 171.

f) The dissociation between the conjugal act and procreation, contrary to the entire tradition of the Catholic Church, from Scripture (*Gn* 1:28) to the present day.[224]

g) Ethical and sometimes legal equalisation of all forms of pairing. Thus, not only successive unions, *de facto* unions, without a formal marriage contract, but also unions of persons of the same sex are propagated. Successive unions in fact deny indissolubility. Temporary or probationary cohabitation does not know indissolubility. Same sex unions do not recognise the anthropological meaning of the difference in sexes (*Gn* 1:27; 2:22-24), inherent in the natural understanding of marriage, according to the Catholic faith.

c) The Absence of Faith can Compromise the Intention to Contract a Natural Marriage

173. [*The absence of faith can compromise the intention to celebrate a marriage that includes some of the goods of marriage*]. From the point of view of dogmatic theology, there is reason to doubt that in the case of marriages between "baptised non-believers," according to the typology we have described, a sacrament of faith takes place because of a serious defect of intention to contract natural marriage, presumably as a very possible consequence, *quasi* inherent in the lack of faith, enunciated differently by the last two pontiffs. The lack of faith in the case of the "baptised non-believers," of the aforementioned typology, can be qualified as unequivocal and determinant of the conceptions of life. Therefore, the doubts mentioned by the pontiffs in a generic way can be assumed in their entirety for these cases. It is not possible to desire, pretend or love what is unknown or explicitly rejected.

174. [*Incidence of absence of faith on the natural goods of marriage*]. In Christian marriage, there is a much greater

---

[224] Cf. Vatican II, Apostolic Constitution *Gaudium et spes*, 50; St Paul VI, Encyclical *Humanae vitae* (25th July 1968) esp. 12 : AAS 60 (1968) 488-489.

bond than in any other sacrament, between the creatural and the supernatural reality, between the order of creation and that of redemption: "marriage has been instituted by God the Creator,"[225] and then elevated to the dignity of a sacrament. Given this very close link, it is understood that a modification of the natural reality of marriage, a departure from the creative project, directly affects the supernatural reality, the sacrament. This connection also occurs in the opposite direction, at least in the extreme case of marriages between "baptised non-believers." For the express denial of supernatural reality, the explicit abandonment of faith, sometimes even with a formal act, or the total absence of adherence to the faith, in those baptised but who never personally assumed the faith, places these persons totally at the mercy of current social opinions on matrimonial and family matters; and it blocks their access to the creatural source of marriage.

175. Indeed, if we consider together the dominant cultural axiomatic, previously outlined, and the line of reflection of Benedict XVI in his last address to the Roman Rota (26th January 2013), we can affirm that, in the absence of clear and explicit faith, the intention with respect to the essential goods of marriage suffers a serious detriment. Benedict XVI has clearly illustrated this with regard to the good of the spouses. His starting point was as follows: "In the context of the Year of Faith, I would like to reflect in particular on several aspects of the relationship between faith and marriage, noting that the current crisis of faith, which is affecting various parts of the world, brings with it a crisis of the conjugal society."[226] In other words, the supernatural element directly affects the natural reality. And he continues later:

---

[225] International Theological Commission, *Propositions on the Doctrine of Christian Marriage* [1977] chapter 3.

[226] Benedict XVI, *Address to the Tribunal of the Roman Rota*, 26th January 2013, § 1: AAS 105 (2013) 168.

It escapes no one that the basic decision of each person to enter into a lifetime bond, influences the basic view of each one according to whether or not he or she is anchored to a merely human level or is open to the light of faith in the Lord. It is only in opening oneself to God's truth, in fact, that it is possible to understand and achieve in the concrete reality of both conjugal and family life the truth of men and women as his children, regenerated by Baptism.[227]

176. The truth of man in natural marriage belongs to God's plan. Benedict XVI links the sacrificial capacity of true generous love, good of the spouses, to openness to true love, which is God, with the intimate unity between truth and love. For the specific love of the good of the spouses to be given, it is necessary to be open to the ultimate truth of love, that is, to the love of God. In a society that proclaims personal self-realisation as the supreme good, it seems very difficult that in the notable and explicit absence of faith the conjugal bond is understood from sacrificial love. In the words of Benedict XVI: "'He who abides in me, and I in him, he it is that bears much fruit, for apart from me you can do nothing' (*Jn* 15:5). This is what Jesus taught his disciples, reminding them of the human being's essential inability to do what is necessary for achieving his true good alone."[228] The understanding of life and the practise of love as unselfish self-transcendence, which seeks first of all the good of the other person, is perfected with divine grace.

177. Sacrificial love and unselfish self-transcendence are not confined to the reciprocal good of the spouses, but they fully affect the good of the offspring, the splendid fruit of the fecundity of conjugal love. If the good of love between the spouses is damaged at its root, it cannot but also directly and explicitly affect the good of the offspring.

---

[227] Benedict XVI, *Address to the Tribunal of the Roman Rota*, 26th January 2013, § 2: AAS 105 (2013) 169.

[228] Ibid.

178. The lack of faith itself includes serious doubts about indissolubility in our cultural context. The deeply ingrained social way of understanding the marriage bond is highly desirable in its permanence, but clearly reviewable in the understanding of what is a proper bond; and the sadly abundant proliferation of separations, means that, without specific source of knowledge, faith as a means of adherence to God's creative plan, there are reasons to doubt that there is a true intention of indissolubility of the bond upon marriage.

179. In short, we have articulated these points. Faith determines very fundamentally the anthropology that is lived. The substantial reality of marriage is anthropological, creatural. A total absence of faith also determines anthropology and, with it, the natural reality of marriage, which is more at the mercy of the dominant cultural axiomatic. A lack of faith of this calibre in this context makes it possible to doubt, on good grounds, the existence of a true natural marriage, which is the indispensable basis on which sacramental marriage is based. In other words, in the case of the "baptised non-believers" described, due to the lack of faith, the intention to enter into a natural marriage cannot be assumed to be guaranteed, nor can it be excluded in the first place.

180. [*From Sacramentality*]. This point of view is in full conformity with the conception of sacramentality which we have been defending (cf. esp. § 16). Let us remember that this consists in the *inseparable correlation* between a visible, external reality, the signifier, and another of a supernatural, invisible, signified nature. The conception of Catholic marriage is based on this understanding of sacramentality. Therefore, for sacramental marriage to take place, a kind of love is required as an external visible reality which, by its particular qualities (goods of marriage: GS 48-50), together with the help received by grace, can signify the love of God. In other words, a marital bond which does not include indissolubility, fidelity, and the

sacrificial disposition towards the other spouse, and openness to offspring would not be a sign capable of signifying Christ's love for the Church. The Church understands that in this type of bond the truth of married love does not emerge.

181. [*Conclusion*]. Our proposal rejects two extremes. On the one hand, we reject an absolute sacramental automatism (cf. esp. §§ 41 e and 78 e), which holds that every marriage between the baptised would be a sacrament, either through the presence of a minimal faith linked to the "character" of baptism or through the intervention of Christ and the Church presupposed by baptism. On the other hand, we reject an elitist sacramental scepticism that holds that any degree of absence of faith would vitiate the intention and thus invalidate the sacrament. We affirm that, in the case of an absence of faith as explicit and clear as that of the described "baptised non-believers," serious doubts about an intention that includes the goods of natural marriage, as understood by the Church, make it possible to maintain serious reservations about the existence of a sacramental marriage. It is therefore consistent with the Church's sacramental practise to deny the sacrament of marriage to those who request it under these conditions, as John Paul II has already held (cf. §§ 153 and 169).

182. [*Pastoral Care*]. Both the cultural context described (cf. §§ 156, 170-172) and the existence of marriages between "baptised non-believers" are a stimulus for the pastoral care of marriage to unfold all its vigour and potential, in line with the suggestions of Pope John Paul II and Pope Francis.[229] The radiance of the profound humanity that is witnessed in Christian families, whose heart is the faith lived by all its members, will be a beacon and a star capable of attracting and convincing. One of its objectives could be precisely these marriages of "baptised non-believers,"

---

[229] Cf. St John Paul II, Apostolic Exhortation *Familiaris consortio* (22nd November 1981) esp. "IV. Pastoral Care of the Family: Stages, Strucures, Agents and Situations": AAS 74 (1982) 158-187; Francis, Apostolic Exhortation *Amoris laetitia* (19th March 2016) esp. "VI. Some Pastoral Perspectives": AAS 108 (2016) 390-415.

since an awakening of faith would mean the emergence of the force of sacramental grace. In any case, the best response to the "desire for family" that, despite the difficulties, is lived everywhere is "the joy of love experienced by families."[230]

---

[230] Francis, Apostolic Exhortation *Amoris laetitia* (19th March 2016) 1: AAS 108 (2016) 311.

5. CONCLUSION: THE RECIPROCITY BETWEEN FAITH AND SACRAMENTS IN THE SACRAMENTAL ECONOMY

183. [*Sacramental Visibility of Grace*]. The sacramental economy, as an incarnational economy, requires of itself a visibility of grace. The Church, heiress and continuer of Christ's work, constitutes this visible sign in history. Its meaning is not reduced to procuring the means of salvation for the faithful themselves. It makes God's saving grace visible in the world. If the Church were to disappear, the historical tangibility of salvation in Jesus Christ would vanish. For this reason, the Church itself renders a service for all. The Church is the means and instrument that proclaims the presence in the history of the universal plan of salvation in Jesus Christ. Every Christian participates in this ecclesial mission, which each sacrament strengthens in its own way. In each sacrament there is a reception of God's gift; there is a configuration with Christ and an ecclesial mission for the life of the world.

184. Since the sacramental sphere refers to external and verifiable visibility, when access to the sacrament is denied, for example in the case of divorced and remarried or others, no conclusion can be drawn from there on the whole truth about the quality of that person's faith. Christians of other Christian denominations are not in full visible sacramental communion with the Catholic Church, because of the persistence of profound differences in Christian doctrine and life. For this reason, the sacramental celebration cannot make visible a full communion.[231] However, it is not excluded on principle that the union with Christ of a non-Catholic Christian, through charity and prayer, may be more intense than that of a Catholic, despite the fact that the

---

[231] For extraordinary cases, cf. CIC, canon 844, § 5 and CCEO, canon 671, § 5; The Pontifical Council for Promoting Christian Unity, *Directory for the Application of Principles and Norms on Ecumenism* (25th March 1993), §§ 122-131.

latter enjoys the objective fulness of the means of salvation. As the liturgy affirms, the ultimate judgement about the quality of each person's faith belongs to God alone: "whose faith and devotion are known to you."[232]

185. [*Growth, Catechumenate*]. Faith, as a virtue, is a dynamic reality. It can grow, strengthen, and mature; but also experience its opposites. The catechumenate helps the reception of the sacraments with a more conscious faith about what is received and about one's personal commitment to it. Pastoral charity will have to decide the concrete terms of the catechumenate according to the sacrament in question and the persons who ask for it, taking into account the quality and intensity of the religious background from which they come. The formation of catechists and their testimony of life are crucial. On the other hand, the very reception of the sacrament, with the commitment it implies, invites us to continue the catechumenate, through mystagogical catechesis, certainly after the sacraments of initiation and marriage. Growth in faith and a kind of continuous catechumenate are aptly given in some of the so-called new ecclesial movements. In them, there is a socialisation achieved in faith and in ecclesial belonging. Moreover, in them the sacramental dimension of faith is strongly emphasised, through the emphasis on the grateful reception of the gift, adoration of the Lord, the frequent reception of the sacraments, emphasising above all the irrevocable gift of God, which binds his grace to the sacraments without conditioning it to the perfection of the ministers or to the merits of those who receive them. From the vertical horizon of sacramentality, they are strengthened, for they do not rely on themselves to give horizontal witness before the world how God's grace makes its way into weakness (*2 Cor* 12:9).

186. [*Insertion into the Sacramental Economy through Faith and the Sacraments*]. The Christian's insertion into the

---

[232] Roman Missal, Eucharistic Prayer I.

sacramental economy happens through faith and the sacraments. The sacraments offer to those who desire it and are adequately disposed something as valuable as the pledge of eternal life and loving closeness of Christ.

187. In the realisation of the sacramental economy, as the unfolding of the incarnation and its logic, the paschal mystery is highlighted as the culmination in which love is realised to the extreme (*Jn* 13:1; 15:13). The Christian, through baptism (the sacrament of faith) is incorporated into this mystery, participating in the death and resurrection of Jesus in a sacramental way (*Rom* 6:3-4); and at the same time, he becomes the living stone of the Church. Thus, Christian life begins with insertion into the essential nucleus of the sacramental economy.

188. The mystery of Christ included in his gift of his Spirit, as the great gift of the Risen One. At Pentecost, with the reception of the Spirit, at the culmination of her own constitution, the Church was fully aware of being graced and sent for a universal mission. The Christian is incorporated into the Pentecostal event through the sacraments of initiation, with a strengthening of his faith and of his responsibility both *ad intra* of the ecclesial community and *ad extra* as a "missionary disciple."

189. At the Last Supper, Jesus anticipated in gestures and words the meaning of his whole life and of his own mystery: his body was given and his blood was shed for the "many." In the Eucharist, the Christian again receives the gift of the Lord, which he expressly accepts as such in the "Amen," in order to continue himself to be an active member of the body of Christ present in the world.

190. The dynamics of the sacramental economy can be read as God's covenant with his people, an image to which the nuptial connotations are not alien. In the whole of the mystery of Christ, the definitive and irrevocable renewal of the covenant of God with his people takes place through Christ. Christian spouses, by

marrying "in the Lord," become a sign that testifies to the love that presides over Christ's relationship with the Church.

191. With his life, death and resurrection, Jesus brought God's salvation, which includes the forgiveness of sins, reconciliation with God, and reconciliation between brothers by breaking down the wall of separation (*Eph* 2:4-6, 11-14). When the Christian contradicts the meaning of the Gospel and the following of Christ, by receiving the sacrament of penance with a repentant faith he is reconciled with God and with the Church. Thus, if on the one hand the Church is renewed, the forgiven one becomes an ambassador of God's forgiveness in Jesus Christ.

192. Jesus approached many sick people, comforted them, healed them and forgave their sins. The one who receives the anointing is sacramentally united to Christ at this moment when the power of sickness and death seems to triumph, to proclaim from faith the victory of Christ and the hope of eternal life.

193. Jesus gathered around him a group of disciples and followers, whom he was instructing in the mysteries of the kingdom of God and manifesting the mystery of his person. Those who respond in faith to the Lord's call and receive the sacrament of Holy Orders are configured with Christ, as Head and Shepherd, to continue proclaiming the Gospel, leading the community in the likeness of the Good Shepherd and offering the living and holy sacrifice.

194. [*Sacramental nature of faith*]. The divine economy of salvation begins with creation, is realised in history, and moves toward eternal consummation. However, not every look at history captures in it the presence of God's action; for example, it may not capture that the departure from Egypt was deliverance wrought by God. Likewise, one can know that Jesus performed miracles or that he was crucified, but only the look of faith recognises in the miracles signs of his messianic nature (cf. *Lk* 7:18-23) and his divinity (cf. *Mt* 14:33; *Lk* 5:8; *Jn* 5), not the power of Beelzebub (cf.

Mk 3:22); or it may not capture that on the Cross the forgiveness of sins took place (cf. *Mt* 27:39-44), along with reconciliation with God (*2 Cor* 5:18-20) and not only an execution.

195. Therefore, following Augustine and Origen,[233] we can distinguish what we can call a simply historicist look at the events of salvation history. It is characterised by limiting itself to the knowledge of the events, by giving credibility to the witnesses who narrate them, but without grasping their historical-salvific meaning. However, the gaze proper to faith, through the gift of the Holy Spirit, not only knows the historical events in their historical materiality, but also perceives in them their salvific nature. In other words, this gaze penetrates into the authentic sacramental reality of what is happening. By grasping the visibility of the historical, it perceives the depth of grace present and acting in these events. This form of faith, which is properly the Christian faith, is responsible not only for capturing the presence of divine action in visible history, but also for the ability to perceive the connection of these events with hope in the future life. Therefore, this kind of faith does not only believe in eternal life, in the Holy Trinity and in Christ our Lord, but it is also the type of faith proper to the persons who recognised the Risen One in the apparitions. Without this faith, history does not take the form of a divine economy of salvation; it is resolved in an accumulation of facts whose meaning is difficult to discern; in any case, it is attributed to it from the outside. However, with the gift of faith, the meaning of the course of historical events lies in the meaning that God himself gives them: the divine economy presides over and governs history, leading it to eternal life. In a word, since the divine Trinitarian economy is of a sacramental nature, Christian faith is genuinely sacramental.

---

[233] Cf. Augustine, *De vera rel.* 50, 99 (CCSL 32, 251); Augustine, *De Trinitate*, I, 6, 11 ; II, 17, 29; IV, 3, 6 (CCSL 50, 40; 119-120; 166-169); *Enarr. in Ps.* 65, 5 (CCSL 39, 842-844); *Ep.* 120, 3, 15; 147 (PL 33, 459; 596-622); Origen, *Com Rm.* 2, 14 (PG 14, 913ff) ; *Hom. in Lc.* 1, 4 (SCh 87, 104-106).